# CrowdFund Your StartUp!

## Raising Venture Capital Using New Crowdfunding Techniques

## Rupert M. Hart

Published by CordaNobeloMedia
Version 1.0 April 20 2012 (10)
Version 2.0 April 27 2012 (36)
Version 2.1 May 7 2012 (52)
Version 2.2 May 9 2012 (59)
Version 2.3 May 21 2012 (81)
Version 2.4 May 24 2012 (87)
Version 2.5 May 29 2012 (92)
Version 2.6 May 30 2012 (93)
Version 2.7 June 12 2012 (100)
Version 2.8 Feb 2 2013 (105)
Version 2.9 Feb 3 2014 (107)
Version 2.91 Feb 4 2014 (108)
Version 2.92 Feb 12 2014 (109)
Version 3.0 Jan 2 2016 (114)
Version 3.01 Jan 18 2016 (117)

Disclaimer: The author provides no professional legal, financial, regulatory or investment services in this book or elsewhere. The author and the publisher do not accept any liability for the information contained here-within. You are advised to seek professional advice.

**Acknowledgements**
Special thanks to: David Fullmer, Colin Palombo, Kevin Lee, Angela Hey, Eppa Hite, Max, Torsten and ex-wife Marie.

## Praise for "CrowdFund Your StartUp"
**(from reviews on amazon.com)**

"With pragmatic wisdom, brutal honesty and a dose of wicked vulgarity, Rupert Hart takes the budding entrepreneur through the challenges of getting a startup funded. If you think that crowdfunding is easy - then think again - this book will teach you to approach your funders professionally. It will give you insights into how venture investors think."

"One of the first accessible resources for those interested in crowdfunding. The prose is very accessible with engaging examples to support the major points."

"The book has everything you need to know legally, a great resource list at the back, and includes the actual JOBS Act."

"I found Rupert Hart's latest book extremely informative and helpful. This book was well written, concise and easy to follow."

"What I like about Rupert Hart is his writing style. Unlike so many authors who write dry and hard-to-digest financial guidance books, Mr. Hart's prose makes you want to keep reading."

"This book is very well researched and the concepts are clearly described. It is also extremely timely. I highly recommend this excellent book."

## Praise for "Recession Storming,"
**(from reviews on amazon.com)**

*"I loved this book! Chock-full of practical, insightful and resourceful tips for helping your company thrive. Hart's book is easy to read with a massive amount of real-world examples. It is well organized with a very detailed table of contents and index." Entrepreneur.*

*"A neat compendium of very practical advice... all in an engaging writing style. Neat stuff, timely advice." Professor Niraj Dawar, Richard Ivey School of Business, Canada.*

"I found this book extremely helpful for my business. It's easy-to-read format made it a quick read. I liked the conversational style and the short paragraphs." Entrepreneur.

"Straightforward, no-nonsense, practical." Business Consultant.

"Wonderfully easy to ready and understand. I love the practical ideas." Property Entrepreneur.

"This is a great business book and immensely timely. I recommend it highly. It's full of actionable ideas that business owners can use today." Chairman, Worldwide Consulting Company.

"As a Harvard MBA, I found this book quite refreshing. While most business books take 200 pages this one contains kernels of wisdom in nearly each paragraph, and packs a wallop in a short, tight read." Serial Entrepreneur.

"The beauty of the book is the many examples and practical ideas. In addition Hart's writing style and compact presentation means the ideas are enjoyably accessible on a long plane flight." Operations Manager.

"An accessible and easily digested book...The straightforward organization of the book and summary headings help the reader grasp the main points without extraneous verbiage. I especially recommend this book for small business owners and young companies." Business Consultant.

"This book is a tool kit of sharp ideas born of practical experience. I have run several small businesses, and I wish such wisdom had been available to me earlier." Entrepreneur.

"Mr. Hart uses ingenious examples and metaphors to make his book understandable, instructive and highly enjoyable." Law Firm Partner.

# Author Background

Rupert Hart is uniquely positioned to write this book, a subject which requires an unusual overlap of experience in entrepreneurial finance, investing and running startups. The key to understanding the implications of Equity Crowdfunding for Startups is seeing the entrepreneurs' point of view as well as the investors' viewpoint.

Rupert worked with Hermann Hauser, founder of ARM Holdings, the $9bn company that designs the chips for the iPhone. He worked closely with Hermann to grow a small startup into the UK part of E*Trade, which revolutionized stock investing for many people around the world; the start-up was later sold to E*Trade for over $200m. He worked with famed product development company IDEO on new ventures. He has worked at Bain & Co on valuations of companies. He has run and advised several startups, and was "Entrepreneur in Residence" at several incubators.

He set up a large network of over 2000 Digital Entrepreneurs. He worked with angel investing groups including International Angel Investors. He has taught micro IPO seminars on 504 and Reg A direct public offerings. He consulted at Amadeus Capital, a high-tech VC firm, and has helped entrepreneurs with their funding through RocketVC.com. Rupert has appeared in the International Herald Tribune, The Daily Mail, and BBC TV's "Business Breakfast" program. He holds an MBA from INSEAD, one of the world's top business schools, where he started the "Entrepreneurial Drinking Club."

Rupert is CEO of ExperiVentures Inc. and works in Silicon Valley. He is the author of "Recession Storming: Thriving in Downturns through Superior Marketing, Pricing and Product Strategies" which was #1 in books on "Recession" on Amazon.com for 3 years. In his spare time he makes large sculptures for the leading-edge Burning Man Arts Festival. He can be reached at Rupert@RupertHart.com.

# Foreword by Jack Burkhart

Entrepreneurs are the lifeblood of America and we should do our utmost to support you! Crowdfunding could well transform the way entrepreneurs are funded. Rupert Hart is right that this new movement has the ability to bring back the American Dream, supply jobs and opportunities for millions of Americans, and provide a useful investment avenue for investors crying out for better returns. Economic booms are often accompanied by new methods of investing, and I think this could be it! Start taking advantage of crowdfunding now!

I am honored to be able to introduce the very first book on this important subject!

*Jack Burkhart is the author of numerous inspirational books for Entrepreneurs, including "The Quotable Entrepreneur," "Shake the Damned Tree," "Fortune Favors the Bold," and "1001 Inspirational Quotes for Entrepreneurs."*

# Contents

.

# Preface to January 2016 Edition

This is it! Ok, almost it!

The SEC has finally published their "final rules" of "Regulation Crowdfunding" with a start date of May 16, 2016. At last, you will be able to raise money over the internet for investors, much larger amounts than previously, and as investors, not just purchasers of products or donors.

It's been almost 4 years since then JOBS Act was passed by Congress. At that time, this was the very first book in the US on equity crowdfunding and it held the top spot on amazon in equity crowdfunding for a year. As you can see, it has been updated several times since then.

Equity CrowdFunding will make a big difference and this book helps to put it all in perspective for a business owner, in a way other books do not. It is a heck of lot easier to read a short book like this of under 100 pages than wade your way through 685 pages of the SEC version. Certainly to start with, while you get used to unfamiliar terminology. It applies to both startups and small businesses which want to grow. I hope you find it uscful.

The book is structured in 5 main parts:
1. How Crowdfunding for Startups Works
2. Setting up a Company Worth Funding
3. Raising the Cash
4. You have the Cash– Now What?
5. The Future of Crowdfunding for Startups

# Preface to February 2014 Edition

Finally, things are beginning to happen and Equity CrowdFunding is about to go live in the US, at last. While signed into law by Congress in 2012, the whole subject has been held up, as you may know, by the need for the Securities and Exchange Commission (SEC) to provide detailed rules for its implementation. Until it does, it is not yet legal to equity crowdfund your startup in the manner of the JOBS Act.

A new Chairman of the SEC, emphasis from the Office of the President, and demonstrated progress made abroad has led to two recent changes you need to be aware of:

1. The SEC has allowed advertising for accredited investors. While this is in no way "general solicitation" where you can market your deal to any investors, it does represent a start.

2. The SEC has finally completed a consultation period and has "committed" to publishing a ruling in the next few months. The SEC has not covered itself with glory over the last few years and has been consistently late on many rulings. Whether the SEC will allow all the terms of the crowdfunding part of the JOBS Act without significant restrictions, and whether it will rule shortly, we will have to wait to find out. My view is that the whole world of investing for shares in startups is about to change very profoundly and this book will be a useful primer.

# Preface to Previous Editions

This book is aimed at you, the entrepreneur, looking for capital to start your company. This book deals specifically with Equity Crowdfunding, where you sell shares in your company. This differs from the usual crowdfunding where you pre-sell products at a discount to early buyers.

I believe this is the real thing: that crowdfunding through the JOBS Act (aka. "equity crowdfunding," otherwise known as Title III) will totally shake up the way startups raise capital. Those entrepreneurs who have used venture capital in the past, the precious few, don't need a book like this. Nor do angel investors who have done a few deals. This book is for entrepreneurs who have not done traditional fundraising; it will help them understand why this is a big deal, how things work, what limitations exist, and why investors want to invest.

Some ways of raising capital are going to change dramatically, and some are going to stay the same. The key is to figure out which are which. Crowdfunding will not replace all the existing methods of raising capital, but it has the potential to totally reconfigure how things are done. Just look at what crowdfunding has done for projects, and think what it could do for raising startup capital:
- *The Pebble* customizable watch. Raised $10.2m.
- *Double Fine* adventure game. Raised $3.3m.
- *Vere* Sandals. Raised $56k.

Is it hyperbole to suggest this might be a once-in-a-generation event? Small changes can have a big effect. For example, venture capital really took off after several minor events: a 1973 law that required companies to set aside money for their employee's pensions, a 1979 relaxation of that law allowing better access to startups for pension funds, and (arguably) a reduction of capital gains tax in 1978. An enormous release of funds occurred, transforming Boston's Route 128 and Silicon Valley. Could the JOBS Act and equity crowdfunding do the same? You be the judge.

Investors have seen the phenomenal wealth effect of those able to invest in Facebook (from startup to $104bn in 10 years) and want to be part of that for other companies. No intermediaries will now stand in their way. They want to believe you can be the next Instagram (3 years to $1bn valuation). This is the entrepreneur's opportunity of a lifetime, and investors want to have a part in it.

In the end, as an entrepreneur, what matters is whether you can make the system work for you. Peter Drucker, renowned management expert and author of "Innovation and Entrepreneurship," wrote that change causes opportunity. I believe that it is time to seize this change.

Enjoy!

# 1.

## How Crowdfunding
## for
## Startups works

Crowdfunding has been around for some years. Raising capital by selling shares for startups is not new either. What is new...is sex between the two, and explosive it is! Liquidity is their love child.

Such "Equity Crowdfunding", with its new implications from recent regulatory changes in Title III of the JOBS Act, is about to provide revolutionary opportunities for entrepreneurs, investors and the service providers who bring them together. This book, quickly and simply, gives you the background for understanding and taking advantage of the crowdfunding cosmos.

Equity crowdfunding, the subject of this book, is a new way of raising venture capital for your startup that is almost but not quite a backdoor IPO. It has all the benefits of a Direct Public Offering of the early 2000s (many small investors) but without the actual aggravation of being public (vast reporting requirements and fees) and of requiring expensive intermediaries. I think this new incarnation of venture capital, combining many hybrid elements of existing financial structures, has evolved into something with revolutionary effect.

It's hard to believe how difficult it was in the past for entrepreneurs to raise capital. You couldn't tell anyone except for your closest family and friends, you had to use an intermediary to approach anyone, your investors had to be proven wealthy with net worth above most of the rest of us. What a nightmare! When you got a bit bigger you could find angel investors. Maybe even banks would be interested in helping you. But let's hope you never had more than 500 investors or you would be in trouble and would have to go public, with all the incredible investment in management time and documentation.

Due to the challenging economy, investing in growth opportunities has been exceptionally difficult over the last few years, and Crowdfunding is a way to break away from lackluster returns. Bringing entrepreneurs and investors together has never been more important than it is now, with the need for trust and vast information flows among many participants who will never meet.

You, the Entrepreneur, are the engine of the money machine, making it all happen. The entrepreneur transforms the startup capital from the investor, produces a product offering which satisfies the customer and makes a profit, in which the investor shares.

Why "crowd"? Glad you asked. The "wisdom of crowds" is a phrase that many of us have heard. It touches a nerve with us because it is the heart of democracy, where everyone has the opportunity to express themselves. Crowds also have power; as when people get together in activist organizations, community societies, or bulk buying clubs, they can achieve things that individuals cannot.

Let's see where all this leads us by examining how we got here.

## How Crowdfunding Came to Be

Crowdfunding for startups has been enabled by the combination of several historical precedents and influences. Equity crowdfunding is a further development of the openness of the Internet. Now you can cut out (or at least reduce the power of) the middlemen and intermediaries with their closed ways of doing things. These are powerful forces and it is useful to mull over them because the future is very fluid and other influences will come in to shape events. Crowdfunding's three most important influences are probably:
1. Small payments such as in micro lending,
2. Payments and information over the Internet, and
3. Individuals talking to each other via social media.

Let's explore these influencing factors.
- *Micro lending.* The most celebrated example is Grameen Bank in India. Mohammed Yunus, an Economics professor, realized that women in a Bangladeshi village remained in poverty because they could not raise the meager capital needed to buy the materials for stools they sold at just 2 cents each. He lent $27 to 42

15

villagers and made them promise to pay back a little every month. This money allowed the villagers to escape from the clutches of the moneylenders. His money was repaid with interest, and the micro lending market is now worth over $6bn in India alone. Microfinance exemplifies how many small donations can make a big difference.

- *Internet payments and information* - EBay/Craigslist and their competitors allow many individuals to make money in small amounts by selling products and services over the Internet. Information is easily transferred from person to person.

- *Social media* - Facebook/Yelp/Amazon Reviews. By allowing individuals to hear about opportunities when their friends "like" and comment on a business, and then being able to forward those leads to others, Facebook and its competitors allow information-sharing among affinity groups. Having access to reviews on Yelp, AngiesList, Amazon reviews, or even LinkedIn, enables us to learn from others' thoughts and experiences.

**Crowdfunding was first used for lending, projects and causes.** Crowdfunding for startups is the latest extension. Let's see how we got here. In deepest darkest history, the term "crowdfunding" was supposedly originated by Michael Sullivan. Business crowdfunding as a concept was then publicized by Paul Spinrad in a post on *Boing Boing*. Before it became used for equity funding (the subject of this book), it had three main incarnations:

1. *Peer-to-peer lending*. Zopa, the world's first peer-to-peer lending organization, was started in the UK in 2005. The Lending Club in the US, now with John Mack, former CEO of Morgan Stanley on its board, has lent over $600m in average loans of $11,000. While several players have exited the market over bad loans, peer-to-peer lending has achieved some good successes.

2. *Raising money for political campaigns and causes*. Perhaps the best known use of Crowdfunding for this purpose has been the Obama political campaign in 2007-2008 when many people from all over the USA were able to donate small amounts of money over the Internet using Facebook. A great number of $20 donations were widely acknowledged as a major factor in Obama's successful presidential campaign.

3. *Raising money for projects.* The best known platforms have been kickstarter.com and indiegogo.com. Some of the biggest successes have been game designers raising money for their projects. Here's how they work:

The originator lists his or her project, the prices for subscription, as well as the amount sought in total, and the deadline. Let's say you want to raise $10K for an art project. Or let's say you want to sell lighted art products and need $5K to get the production line going. You could sell a package of 5 products for $20, a package of 10 for $50, and so on. The purchaser accesses the website, transfers money to the escrow account. He then waits to hear whether the project meets the target funding threshold. If not, the money is returned. If the project successfully raises enough capital, then the originator will deliver the product to the purchaser.

It's important to note that these platforms, when used for projects, typically allow two options: a. you get all the money sent to you, or, b. you get no money at all until you reach your target. When it comes to startups, however, only b. is allowed under the JOBS Act. Here is how it works for Crowdfunding:

If the project does not reach a threshold target goal of funds raised, all the money is returned. From the entrepreneur's point of view (for startups and small projects) this is unfortunate. The entrepreneur could still start, get going, and then demonstrate success before returning to raise more money. This is, of course, an investor safeguard that prevents chronically underfunded ventures being drains on investor funds. After failing the first time, the entrepreneur could restart the process with a lower target amount, but that is so time consuming that judging the right funding target the first time becomes extremely important. My belief is that when it comes to Crowdfunding, the entrepreneur could perhaps publish contingency plans if differing amounts of cash are raised. It is also important to set the threshold at a reachable level, as we will see later.

**What we can learn from Equity Crowdfunding in Europe.**
Several countries in Europe have had crowdfunding platforms to raise venture capital (="equity crowdfunding") for some time. These include Sweden and the UK. The US has now caught up with the JOBS/CROWDFUND Act. We can learn from other countries' experience. Crowdsourcing.org reports that 80% of companies looking for equity raised more than $25,000, which indicates that the sums raised are much larger for equity-based projects than lending, causes and projects, as you might expect.  CrowdFunder.com reports that by 2012, before the US made it legal there, over 14% of all crowdfunding sites around the world were offering equity-funding. There are useful links to European sites at the back of the book.

**How is a company different from projects or causes?**
Crowdfunding for startups is whole new level up from Crowdfunding projects, causes and loans. It's critical to understand why this is. Until now, the purchaser (investor) has not been able to buy a share in the company through Crowdfunding, but only a right to a discounted product or service. Well, the law has now been changed so that is possible. Why is this important and what does this mean for you, the entrepreneur?

The key is to understand how a company is different from a project. Several things come to mind:
- A company exists for several reasons: it minimizes the hassle of finding independent contractors all the time (i.e. reduces "transaction costs"), it limits investors' liability to their investment, it helps build trust with suppliers, and is crucially important for branding.

- A company is a system, made up of people who do things in a process. A system has great value when it works well, and it can produce more and more product-offerings at reduced costs, when managed properly.

- Companies are usually about more than one product, they require more capital, and they work on timescales that tend to be longer than a project.

- Unlike crowdfunded products, which you often buy for yourself at a lower price, a company can produce products an investor might not actually personally want, such as a telecom router chip.

- With a company structure, an entrepreneur can attract people who care about financial returns, unlike a cause. For this, a management team is important. A stable company with a proven management team can make a big difference in profitability – this is important compared to most projects which generally offer low or negative profitability.

## Raising capital for startups before Crowdfunding

For startups, the key is having cash to spend immediately. Before equity crowdfunding, this capital came from these sources:

- *Government grants*. Wow! Doesn't get any better than this. Not so common in the US, but possible to win in Europe. DARPA (Defense Advanced Research Projects Agency) projects always handy, of course.

- *Prizes*. Someone somewhere believes in something strongly enough to offer a large prize, if only you can configure your product-offering to meet the goal.

- *Loans, guaranteed loans and SBA loans*. Sweet-talk your bank into an unsecured loan ("I need a car"), or a Small Business Loan, or a loan guaranteed by your partner's father...or one from a shady Russian character with the whole company's equity as collateral (it's been done and I know the entrepreneur who did this).

- *Savings.* Planning on going on vacation or buying a house? Put it into your startup.

- *Credit cards.* 41% of all startups are funded by credit cards, so get the limits up now!

- *Cashed-out 401ks.* Has to be done sometimes.

- *Released House Equity or Reverse Mortgages.* Isn't your house an ATM already?

- *Promises.* Same as loans but maybe with no hard promises or repayment timescales put on them.

- *Delayed vendor payment terms.* How well do you know your vendors and how well can you persuade them to help you?

- *Options and warrants.* Can't pay your people? Offer them options. Can't pay your consultants? Pay them warrants.

- *FFF: Friends, fools and family.* You believe in yourself. They believe in you. Enough said.

- *Private placements.* OK, beginning to get serious now. A broker gets you to sign serious documents and finds investors to place your offering.

- *Angel investors.* Wealthy investors who sometimes know about investing in startups and/or your industry put in money and help you succeed. They can be entrepreneurs recycling their capital and knowledge, or doctors and dentists looking to pep up their returns and diversify their investments.

- *Convertible debt.* A good idea for many investments: they loan you money on a zero coupon (i.e. no need to make regular payments) and then when the next round is raised from more serious investors, they work backwards to put a retrospective valuation on your company. Rather good.

- *Venture Capital*. The Big Daddy, but also very rare. Often used as the term for all startup capital, but usually the venture capitalists are very demanding.

- *DPOs: Reg D, 504, 505 and 506 exemption, and Nevada corporations*. The Crowdfund Act is not the first time the SEC has granted exemptions to its extensive registration rules. Regulation D and its associated 504, 505 and 506 articles have been available for smaller companies but the number of shareholders and net worth requirements were still quite restrictive. Nevada has long had several additional exemptions. These "Direct Public Offerings" (DPOs) have had disadvantages of restricted location and public company reporting requirements which equity crowdfunding has largely overcome. There is an excellent summary of Rules like 504 on pages 357, 358 of the final rules.

This is how it was. A lot has changed with the JOBS Act and its effect on crowdfunding for startups.

### What is New with the Regulation Crowdfunding and what it will mean
What changed was the JOBS Act of 2012 and the final rules of Regulation Crowdfunding. Among other things, it has massively changed the way entrepreneurs can obtain investment funding, and how investors can reach entrepreneurs through crowdfunding.

To understand why this is a big deal, you have to know how it used to be:
1. As an entrepreneur you just weren't allowed to market your company for investment. It seems almost incredible, but you couldn't tell people you met about your company and how they could invest in it. Well, there was an exception for FFF: friends, fools and family, but besides that, only a certified financial planner

could approach anyone else. It was not legal to place ads anywhere to attract investors.

2. You could only sell shares to people who were high net worth or accredited investors. Well if you are only looking for a small amount of money and small amounts from each person, then it seems crazy that you were only allowed to have wealthy or knowledgeable investors, but that's how it was.

3. You were only allowed to have less than 500 investors. This may not seem much of an issue, but if you ever get big you might have more than 500 people wanting to be investors. After that you would be forced to go public, with the enormous expenses associated with that effort. This can become an important consideration if the number of employees in your company grows quickly!

**Commentary of the final rules of Regulation Crowdfunding**

Firstly, a quick perusal shows that Regulation Crowdfunding is a series of exemptions to previous laws from 1933 governing securities. As you can imagine, those 1933 and 1934 regulations were set up to protect investors after the Great Crash. These exemptions have the basis that the opportunities in funding startups outweigh the risks of investor fraud, seeing as they can be managed to be smallish transactions. That's the theory, anyway, and it is worth bearing that in mind when you read blogs about the subject.

There are three main "players" in a transaction: the investor, the intermediary (broker-dealer or portal), and the issuer (that's you, the start-up). This is the language used by the SEC.

The final rules are rather longwinded and, if you are new to raising equity, a bit complicated. It's also hard to see what is important and make sure you understand that first, before getting into the nitty-gritty. So here is a summary of the really important stuff:

1. *Maximum Issue $1m*. The maximum raise in a 12 month period is $1m. Note that this includes fees paid to the broker-dealer or portal. This means the net funds will be less than $1m. You can see that they are trying to make Crowdfunding work, but not to let deals get so big they cause big problems.

   *An issuer is permitted to raise a maximum aggregate amount of $1 million through crowdfunding offerings in a 12-month period;*

2. *Reduced investor net worth requirements*. This is big and really new. For the first time ever, people like you and me will be able to invest, without having a million in assets. There are two levels of investor. And there is a requirement on the intermediary to make sure the investor does not invest more than $100,000 in one year across all crowdfunded deals.

   *Individual investors, over the course of a 12-month period, are permitted to invest in the aggregate across all crowdfunding offerings up to:*
   1. *If either their annual income or net worth is less than $100,000, then the greater of: $2,000 or 5 percent of the lesser of their annual income or net worth.*
   2. *If both their annual income and net worth are equal to or more than $100,000, then 10 percent of the lesser of their annual income or net worth; and*
   *Additionally, during the 12-month period, the aggregate amount of securities sold to an investor through all crowdfunding offerings may not exceed $100,000.*

3. *Funding Portals or Brokers required*. You are required to go through a funding portal or broker-dealer. And you can only choose one. They need to be registered with a national securities association, and they cannot market your deal to potential investors, nor can they hold onto your investor's cash. There are also some large paragraphs about what they can and can't say and do, in terms of information to potential investors.

4. *Must meet Target Funding Threshold.* Your company doesn't get any of the money unless you reach the target funding threshold. If you don't make it, you have to refund all the money. This is much like KickStarter and IndieGoGo and is designed to prevent companies not really starting up, floundering around in an undercapitalized state and then slowly dying. This means you need to choose your price and your target raise very carefully.

5. *Limitations on commissions for brokers.* As a privacy concern, you will not be allowed to compensate promoters and lead generators for providing personal information to the broker or funding portal. This implies a separation of marketing and managing funds. [See page H.R. 3606-12.]

6. *Reduced financial reporting standards.* Reducing the requirements for financial reporting has reduced the enormous costs there used to be. It seems that you can escape the onerous Sarbanes-Oxley and Dodds-Frank reporting and corporate governance requirements. But you can be sure investors will be wary of less supervision: it might be an idea to go up to the next level of financial reporting, even if you don't have to. As Groupon has seen, it might pay to have high level financial people on board earlier rather than later. There are three levels:
   a. Less than $100k issued in 12 months: company officer can certify the accounts.
   b. Between $100k and $500k issued in 12 months: a public accountant needs to review the accounts.
   c. More than $500k issued in 12 months: accounts need to be audited.

   *For background, a review is a limited check of the financials by an accountant. It basically says, "I haven't seen anything wrong here." An audit, on the other hand, is a proactive check where the accountant tests inputs and opines on the accuracy of the financial statements.*

*For issuers offering $100,000 or less: disclosure of the amount of total income, taxable income and total tax as reflected in the issuer's federal income tax returns certified by the principal executive officer to reflect accurately the information in the issuer's federal income tax returns (in lieu of filing a copy of the tax returns), and financial statements certified by the principal executive officer to be true and complete in all material respects. If, however, financial statements of the issuer are available that have either been reviewed or audited by a public accountant that is independent of the issuer, the issuer must provide those financial statements instead and need not include the information reported on the federal income tax returns or the certification of the principal executive officer.*

*• Issuers offering more than $100,000 but not more than $500,000: financial statements reviewed by a public accountant that is independent of the issuer.352 If, however, financial statements of the issuer are available that have been audited by a public accountant that is independent of the issuer, the issuer must provide those financial statements instead and need not include the reviewed financial statements.*

*• Issuers offering more than $500,000:*
*o For issuers offering more than $500,000 but not more than $1 million of securities in reliance on Regulation Crowdfunding for the first time: financial statements reviewed by a public accountant that is independent of the issuer. If, however, financial statements of the issuer are available that have been audited by a public accountant that is independent of the issuer, the issuer must provide those financial statements instead and need not include the reviewed financial statements.*
*o For issuers that have previously sold securities in reliance on Regulation Crowdfunding: financial statements audited by a public accountant that is independent of the issuer.353*

7. *Advertising opened up.* You will be able to advertise the offering and direct potential investors to the funding portal

or broker. You are now allowed to publicize your deal to non-accredited investors. And to people from other states and countries. This is truly an amazing phenomenon that was never allowed before. This general solicitation and general advertising were most certainly not permitted before. If you were to publicize a deal on a website you would previously have to be registered as a broker-dealer, which is not the case now. You can at last go big in telling the world that your startup exists and is looking for money, and you don't have to determine that your audience is accredited investors. Of course, as already seen, before taking investors' money, the broker-dealer or portal will have to make sure they are within the (reduced) net worth thresholds.

*Under the final rules, an advertising notice that includes the terms of the offering can include no more than: (1) a statement that the issuer is conducting an offering, the name of the intermediary through which the offering is being conducted and a link directing the investor to the intermediary's platform; (2) the terms of the offering; and (3) factual information about the legal identity and business location of the issuer, limited to the name of the issuer of the security, the address, phone number and website of the issuer, the e-mail address of a representative of the issuer and a brief description of the business of the issuer. Consistent with the proposal, the final rules define "terms of the offering" to include: (1) the amount of securities offered; (2) the nature of the securities; (3) the price of the securities; and (4) the closing date of the offering period.*

Note also there are some limitations on paying commissions for generating leads:

*..the final rules also specify that the issuer shall not compensate or commit to compensate, directly or indirectly, any person to promote its offerings outside of the communication channels provided by the intermediary, unless the promotion is limited to notices that comply with the advertising rules discussed above*

8. *Lockup period for Investors.* New shareholders are required to hold their shares for a year unless they sell back to the issuer, sell to an accredited investor, sell in an offering, sell to a family member (e.g. in case of death). This is rather handy as it reduces hot money speculating on your deal and then deserting you. It also makes keeping track of investors easier. But it can make share prices volatile.

   *..securities issued in a transaction pursuant to Section 4(a)(6) may not be transferred by any purchaser of such securities during that one-year period unless such securities are transferred: (1) to the issuer of the securities; (2) to an accredited investor; (3) as part of an offering registered with the Commission; or (4) to a member of the family of the purchaser or the equivalent, to a trust controlled by the purchaser, to a trust created for the benefit of a member of the family of the purchaser or the equivalent, or in connection with the death or divorce of the purchaser or other similar circumstance.*

9. *No cap on number of shareholders.* No longer will your company be limited to having 500 investors before it has to go public (now it is 2000). When you are raising on average, say, $500 from investors, it doesn't take much to go over the 500 investor threshold. In which case you would have to find a lot of money and management time before you were really ready. You don't have to worry about that nightmare any more.

   *Holders of these securities would not count toward the threshold that requires a company to register its securities under Exchange Act Section 12(g) if the company is current in its annual reporting obligations, retains the services of a registered transfer agent and has less than $25 million in total assets as of the end of its most recently completed fiscal year.*

10. *Reduced fees*. There will be reduced or no fees for certain filings. This was a major deterrent before, as the fees were crippling.

11. You don't need to be limited to shares, but you can offer debt securities, such as convertible bonds (effectively loans that can be converted to equity.)

    *The final rules do not limit the types of securities that may be offered in reliance on Section 4(a)(6), and thus debt securities may be offered and sold in crowdfunding transactions.*

12. Communications are based around online communications. This saves money and the need to send out large printed documents, which is how it used to be done.

## Good Uses of StartUp Crowdfunding

Here are a few of my thoughts:

- *Companies that need money for growth*. Crowdfunding is best suited for companies that need money to grow. Why? Consider one extreme: you are eBay in the early days, you make vast amounts of money without advertising, and there is so much funding that you don't know what to do with it. There would be no need to take in more money through Crowdfunding. Or another extreme: you are a stable company with a dominant market share and you can't see good growth opportunities, so there would be little you could use the money for.

- *Unfashionable, nontraditional and outrageous areas of investing.* Consider an example. Whatever your political or social views, everybody knows that porn is one of the industries that makes a lot of money on the Internet, and they use their retained earnings to obtain vast marketing resources to increase sales even further. So why not fund a startup with crowdfunding so that it has resources similar to existing companies and get a jump-start on sales? Liquidity could come from gray market sales and dividends.

- *Single product companies.* Hit and run companies that exist only to make one product that has a short life are ideal candidates for crowdfunding. Normally we think of companies as self-perpetuating, but what if you saw an opportunity that was short-lived and could make money quickly? Crowdfunding is the perfect solution for raising capital for this type of venture.

- *Trendy companies that turn venture capital upside-down.* Venture capital companies avoid fashion businesses because they don't feel they have a good handle on trends. Warren Buffett avoids technology companies because he doesn't understand the technology. The Jimmy Choo co-founder and designer had to work with several rounds of venture capitalists who supposedly vetoed her designs of ultra-high heels, which later became a hit for her competitors. Maybe your crowdfunding investors have a better understanding of what people want than venture capitalists do!

- *Incredibly Disruptive Companies.* If you have a totally revolutionary business model that could shake everything up, few existing financiers will take a risk on you, but crowdfunders might set you up to prove the market exists! And then the bigger money will flow.

- *Vendors need a new supplier.* Somebody out there is screwing someone with a monopoly and someone doesn't like it, but not enough to really do something about it themselves. You could get some funding from them, add funding from a crowd, and then make their investment liquid so they wouldn't need to consider this a big commitment.

- *Where returns are much too small for them to bother.* Venture capital firms want to hit the ball out of the park, to achieve 10x their money. This is essential because so many companies don't become hits at all, and because the business model for venture capital firms is based on investing a lot of time in each client. But if Crowdfunding means investors don't need to invest so much time, then they can be happier with lower returns on each of their deals.

- *Young or imperfect teams.* Maybe venture capitalists wouldn't touch you because you're still forming your team, but crowdfunding investors can invest small sums in lots of small startups, however risky. The risk is spread much more thinly.

- *Quick investment is critical.* When the market won't wait, and you can't raise the money fast enough through traditional channels, Crowdfunding is the way to go!

- *When you don't want (or can't get) a loan.* A loan requires consistent repayments, which might be difficult to manage with a growing startup. You might not like the burden of a loan. Or you may not have the assets to back a larger loan. Then Crowdfunding may be useful for you. You can sell the idea to Crowdfunding investors by pointing out that selling shares means the investors get to share the upside.

- *Benefit Corporations.* These newly-created entities might be perfect for equity crowdfunding. They are "do-good" businesses that aim to provide benefits for stakeholders as well as generate financial returns for the shareholders.

## Other Uses of StartUp Crowdfunding

Here are a few of my thoughts on where Crowdfunding might not be your best choice:

- Backdoor to selling out your company
- Obtain working capital
- Fund an acquisition
- Retire debt
- Incredibly high-tech
- Where you don't need quick money
- Immensely capital-intensive ventures

Here's how it works in brief: you establish something worth investing in, raise capital, build the company, then allow the investors to put a price on their investment and exit. Let's look at these in turn.

# Summary:
## 1. How Crowdfunding for Startups works

This is the first time you can sell shares in your company over the Internet to other than wealthy investors.

Crowdfunding was first used for causes, projects and products.

There are many sources of capital for entrepreneurial business; crowdfunding is one more.

***Regulation Crowdfunding's three main advantages are:***
- Now you can market the company's shares,
- You can take money from less wealthy people, and
- The fees are massively reduced.

***Key components of Regulation Crowdfunding are:***
1. You can raise up to $1m a year,
2. You can raise $2k or 5% from anyone earning over $100k and more from wealthier investors,
3. You need to use a licensed funding portal or broker,
4. Your company gets nothing if you don't meet the target funding threshold,
5. You are limited in how you can offer commissions,
6. You have to prepare financial reports but they are simpler than public companies,
7. You can advertise that you company is looking for investment,
8. Investors have some restrictions on how quickly they can sell,
9. You can take money from more than 500 shareholders,
10. There are reduced fees.

# 2.

## Setting up a Company
## Worth Funding

You are going to encounter a lot of competition in your search for funds, so you will need to make sure you have a viable product, a decent team, and a reasonable deal; otherwise you will be wasting time and money and achieve nothing. Now, venture capital investors are somewhat split between whether the first thing to consider is the product or the team. The latter being the school of thought that if you have clever people, then they can re-orient the company towards a workable solution, regardless of the product being developed. You be the judge.

You don't really want to be the 5th producer of a fart app, so do yourself a favor by taking a look at the following:

**Getting the Dogs to Eat the Dog Food**
Obviously you need to have a compelling product or service. There are three aspects you need to consider:

Does your solution meet a real need? Three thoughts:
- *Is this a pain problem, or a pleasure solution?* This is the classic question venture capitalists ask. But maybe, just maybe, the new Crowdfunding changes the rules so much that it doesn't matter. Maybe people who are investing a few bucks don't care as much as a venture capitalist who will be nurturing the company and spending a lot of time on it. And some people have argued that many consumers in the developed world have few true needs as such, being more desires. Until then, it will certainly be helpful if you are solving a problem that customers perceive needs to be solved or you are providing something that will bring the customers real pleasure, rather than just a "nice to have."

- *Are customers aware of a problem?* Human beings are remarkable coping machines: we can "get used to it" and live with many annoyances. If customers aren't aware of a problem, then they aren't actively searching for a solution and it might be hard for you to reach them. Then again, if you can affordably make them aware of a problem, you may be well ahead of your competitors. Investors will want to see some evidence that this is a big problem: editorial articles, companies or customers making homemade versions to solve their problem, blogs expressing their frustration at the workarounds needed in the current system.

*Do customers accept the product?* If you present the real product to a real-live customer who is in your target segment, will he actually buy? You have got over any issue of him not knowing about it, so now it is all about acceptance. Investors want to see real sales, orders, and letters of intent to purchase. One of the best customer acceptance formulations was devised by Everett Rogers. In its improved form it is:

- o A: advantage: is it better?
- o C: compatible: does it fit with the way things are done now?
- o C: complexity: if it is too complex, nobody wants it
- o T: trialable: can you try it out before you commit?
- o O: observable: can you see the product and its advantages?

## Being Better than the Competition
Three thoughts:

- *Better than existing?* Our worlds are filled with too much information, misinformation, marketing hype and sheer noise. Your product offering needs to be at least 30% better than what is out there. Sometimes several times better. You must overcome customer inertia, and our collective experience that so many new things rarely seem to work as advertised. Is your solution much better? Is the customer saying "Wow!"?

- *Better than substitutes?* It's not just competing products you need to surpass, but also other ways of doing things, or what we might call "substitutes." As the saying goes: What customers want are holes in wood – they don't really care how they get there, whether by buying a drill, buying wood with holes already in it, or hiring someone to drill the hole. We humans can find lots of ways of doing things, and many people have different ways of doing them, so make sure yours is better.

- *Is your product defensible?* OK, so it is a lot better, but if it can easily be copied, then you have a few options: hope that no one will notice or bother with it, stay invisible (by directing your efforts only at certain customers); move rapidly (move onto the next idea or iteration before competitors do); or effect a "hit and run" mentality of just exploiting a small time window.

### Yes, Making Money

In the dotcom days, and in spells of speculative euphoria, there has often been a suspension of the demand on companies to make money. This is usually based on the "greater fool" theory of selling the company to the next investor before the chickens come home to roost. If you are an investor, it might be wiser to invest in a company that has a plan to make money.

A few thoughts:

- *Customer value over costs.* Costs can be slippery and hard to account for. But ultimately, if the customer when right in front of you will only pay a price that won't cover your costs of getting in front of that customer, then unless something changes, all the investor money will be depleted in time, and the more it will go the faster you sell. Obviously, the customer must be willing to pay a decent price and you must have low enough costs to yield a decent positive margin. As a small businessman, I object strongly to losing money on any contract because money is coming from my back pocket and being given to the customer; that's not why I am in business and not why you should be, either.

- *Marketing costs and overheads not overwhelming.* Groupon is a good example of where acquiring customers can so diminish profits that there is little or nothing left. You could regard it as an investment in marketing but there comes a time when the investment is not paying off. For example, Google Adwords or

Yellow Pages can definitely be losing propositions: you pay more for customers than you can make from selling to them.

- *Will it recover its startup costs?* Are massive upfront "investments" really going to pay off, or are they really just big bets on big wins that may never come? Boo.com was perhaps the most celebrated dot bomb of the 2000s; they spent tens of millions of dollars in a brief flash of investment on a fashion website that never made more than $1m revenue before imploding.

## Lifting-off Quickly

Just existing as a company means costs eating away your precious capital. Meanwhile, your investors are thinking about how much their investments could be returning elsewhere. And your team is thinking about their lost opportunities in the outside world. So speed is essential. Three thoughts:

- *Rapid customer awareness*. Though you would like to start at a slow-ish level, trying out an approach and getting it right first, you will need to get customers quickly or you may run out of cash waiting as you struggle to acquire them.

- *Rapid customer acceptance*. It costs money and time to acquire potential leads. Ideally, you want a large number of these targeted leads to buy your product, but if the product offering doesn't meet their needs, then you will have to do a lot of expensive winnowing to find the ones who will buy.

- *Rapid prototyping to get to a winnable solution*. At IDEO we used to say "Fail often in order to succeed sooner." Try lots of little experiments to get a winning formula quickly and then roll it out.

How risky is it? Here are some thoughts;

- *Will your company run out of cash?* Ultimately this is the fate of all companies (unless you become insolvent first, or get bought). But your investors and your team don't want to see this happen!

- *Do you have forgiving margins?* You can be sure your business plan is going to be optimistic, given you are an entrepreneur. That means things are definitely going to be worse than projected. Many unexpected crises will appear; you want to make sure you have enough margin to live on, even under margin compression.

- *Will you overspend before lifting off?* As we have seen above, many companies deplete their funds before they have a winnable solution, and it is usually the fear of imminent crash that leads them to what works...but too late!

**Building the Team**

As an entrepreneur you might be thinking that money is your only real problem, but you may well find that the team is one of your biggest priorities. You will of course be able to pick up better people later on, as you become successful, but investors will judge you by the company you keep, and they will soon likely be inundated with similar companies. They will start looking for ways to differentiate you from the rest, and the main way they will do this will be by your team. It is what venture capitalists do, and your investors will, too.

Aspects of teamwork investors look for are:
- *Have they worked together before?* Teams who are familiar with each other and members' working styles can gel as a new team, making fewer mistakes in the process of forming your company, and this is attractive to investors.

- *Does your team have industry-specific knowledge?* It is true that while skills in analyzing business situations and being able to see your way through to a solution, such as are learned from business school or in other industries, are immensely useful, but there are times when this might not be enough. Each industry has certain ways of doing things, and sometimes there is a good reason for them. Also, how customers and competitors will react is often something you know by

38

intuition when you have been in the industry a bit. Domain knowledge is a useful thing. Of course, you can always hire someone with that knowledge, but the trick is to know when to value it, and when to ignore it!

- *Is your team adaptable enough to cope with unexpected changes?* Things can happen fast and the unexpected is to be expected. You have to be on the lookout for changes and be aware of them before they have a real impact. As a kid I used to sail with my father and he would tell me to brace for a gust in 20 seconds. How did he know a gust was coming? He could see how the water rippled in the near distance as a gust approached the boat. You have to be able to make decisions quickly without complete information. Often people look for qualifications or names of well-respected companies on your resume or those of your team members in order to assure this kind of training and experience in being nimble.

- *Do your team members represent all the main core functions of a management team?* Of course, you can hire people as you get bigger, but the course of the company is often set very quickly by the core team. So is there a complete core team, or do you have a purely technical guy making marketing decisions? You don't need to have a fulltime CFO on board yet, however.

- *Do they have good balance of skills*? Making a company work is a difficult undertaking. Especially when things don't go as planned and money is not pouring in the door. What clues are there that your team can do it?

  o *People skills*: Startups are stressful affairs, people do fall out with each other and the loss of a team member at an early stage can be fatal.

  o *Customer intuition*. We have all seen companies where the guy at the top was, say, a financial guy but had no feeling for customers and canceled critical projects. Bob Lutz wrote about this at GM when it had hideous looking cars nobody wanted to buy because costs had been repeatedly taken out of the budgets by the bean counters who were out of touch with what consumers wanted.

- o *Does the team have sales skills?* We are all selling all the time, and no skill is more important than sales talent at this stage. Persuading the first customer, the first investor, and the first new hire will all require sales skills.

- o *Financial skills.* It doesn't take an accountant to run a company, but having at least the awareness of a household manager doing the weekly grocery shopping would be a good idea. Forgetting that a company is a profit generating machine will lead to trouble eventually.

- o *Feeling for the product.* If you were selling a software product and didn't know anything about software, you could pay for a team with the skills to run the day-to-day operations of the company, but you would never know that a project was massively overdue until it's too late, or you could get blindsided by people who don't share your motivations.

- o *Track record and gray hairs.* The enormous energy, the willingness to try what has never been tried before, and having little to lose mean big advantages for younger people. Combine that with wisdom accumulated over years and many business cycles, experience with other startups, and credibility, and you have the magic elixir that adds up to success for you!

- o *Financial incentives for the team.* Investors want to see that the team has incentives to make the company work  because when the going gets tough, the team starts going, unless you can show they are strongly incentivized to stay. Your investors will want to see that they will stay. Also, many investors like to see that the team has some skin in the game. So they will look for previous time spent on this, money spent in the past, reputational risk, anything that might tie the team to a good result.

- o *A clear leader.* There are few excellent organizations with more than one leader. A sure warning sign to investors is where all three founders have the same equity, role and title. As Luke Johnson says, "most first-time entrepreneurs don't realize that fairness and being nice matter less than relative, tangible contributions [in] stamina, talent and connections."

**Making Your Company Attractive to Investors**
The key for Crowdfunding investors is to find a way to get into startups at the ground level. That's where the opportunity lies. The question for them is access, and avoiding duds.

In the past, it was very difficult for investors to even hear about startups. When they did, they could never be sure that the person was not trying to sell them on a favorite scam. And they heard of so few that they could reasonably ignore all of them as being frauds. Not any more. Now companies can market themselves, and investors are about to be inundated with opportunities.

Even if a potential investor heard about a startup, it was very hard to get in, because they weren't allowed to take just any investor's money, they weren't set up to take their money, and they offered their shares to bigger investors. Now there will be more opportunities and the universe of available options will expand to one that is bigger than can be supplied by all that old capital.

So how do investors avoid a dud? Here are some tried and true techniques that should still be valid: they follow smart capital, and they seek out research and opinions.

## Understanding How Investors Think

Crowdfunding offers the potential of higher returns. Let's face it, if they do nothing, investors' money is not going to be earning much, if anything, after inflation with current low interest rates. Emerging market equities are volatile, currencies don't always increase in value, and the dollar has been gently sinking. Bonds are not going to provide much of a return while the Federal Reserve pumps out funds. Gold and commodities are likely to be oversold. Oil is rather volatile. Shorting means you have to roll over options, which incurs significant expenses. So yield is hard to come by.

*Survival Rates*. We have all heard of the 90% failure rate among new enterprises, of which the vast majority are lifestyle businesses. But it turns out that higher potential firms run by talented and experienced founders have much higher success rates. Small Business Administration statistics (quoted by Bill Bygrave) indicate that after 6 years from startup, a 40% survival rate has been typical. This increases to 78% for high growth companies. This success rate, and the higher returns possible, are what attracts investors.

*Liquidity*. One of the problems of private companies, as opposed to public companies on exchanges, is that the true price of the shares is hard to determine when markets are illiquid, and it is hard to sell up when you want to. What is more, if an investor chooses to sell, and absolutely needs to, he may get a low price, and that price is what is put on your shares. In small illiquid companies, you can see large swings in price. The key is only to invest what you can afford to, and hang on in the expectation of it taking several years or more before you get your money out, if ever.

A friend of mine borrowed a fair sum of money on a credit card at the beginning of 2000 to invest in a startup with good management in a good area with a product that was receiving wild acceptance from business customers. But, the dotcom crash meant there was to be no rapid selloff. The company did survive and even took on more capital and about 5 years later they sold out to another company. The problem was that the terms of the deal were that the bigger investors got twice their money first, and then the other shareholders got to draw on what was left. Unfortunately the well was dry, and these shareholders received nothing, and that was after five years of holding the money at high rates, so beware!

*Taxes*. Don't forget taxes! Capital gains taxes are lower than payroll taxes, but they are due to rise and they can take a substantial chunk out of any gains. You may be thinking that this one will knock the ball out of the court. But what if you are wrong and it just slides along; taxes may take a big chunk out of that!

*Opportunity costs*. When investors assess an opportunity they have to decide whether this one is better than others they may have access to. They could put the money into their house, invest in certificates of deposit, save it at the bank, invest in mutual funds, buy some gold bullion, put it into a 401k, go to college perhaps, or even leave it under their mattress. Each of these opportunities has an expected return, and this opportunity has to be compared with all of those to find the one that is best for them. If they choose to invest in your opportunity and another would have produced better returns, then they will suffer an opportunity cost. Now, of course, since much of life is unknown, they are making an assessment now about the future which they may not be able to correct in midcourse with such an illiquid investment. Inflation is an issue you need to consider, as is recession risk. So it is all down to their selection now.

*Expected Financial Returns*.
Spectacular successes for companies like Facebook, Google, Apple, Lotus, and Digital Equipment are what quickens the heartbeat of investors. The most successful (and well-documented) data are for venture-capital-backed companies. For a group of 218 companies (as reported by Bill Bygrave, see "Resources" at back of this book) 15% resulted in total loss, and 25% partial loss, making 40% involving some loss. 4% returned 10 times the original investment after taxes, and another 8% returned 5 to 10 times. This translates to a 25% compounded return on investment after taxes and is why we are all here.

How do investors look at your company in terms of financial return? In simple terms you could think of investing in an opportunity as a machine into which you put $100 and get out, say $200. That would be a 100% payback. Not bad. Most investors realize that the time it takes to get that payback is important when comparing opportunities. If it took one year to get $200 back, that would be fabulous! But if it took 20 years, that investment might not have been the wisest choice. So most traditional investors, like angel investors and venture capital funds, use IRR, or Internal Rate of Return. In essence it is asking what the effective interest rate would be on an investment, such as depositing it into a bank account. In the case of one year the IRR would be 100%. In the second case, where the payback is 20 years, it would be considerably less. In addition, time means inflation rears its ugly head. If you could put your money into an inflation proof asset like TIPS (Treasury Inflation-Protected Securities) then anything else you put it into instead has an opportunity cost.

And, an investor might take some money out halfway through and then the rest at the end, or he may even receive dividends all the way through, as well. All this complicates the situation.

*Dilution*. Companies rarely raise all the money they will ever need in one round. The reason is that companies are risky things and investors rate them less highly than insiders. Therefore entrepreneurs issue stock in several stages, related to milestones that are linked to the reduction of risks. In many ways, this strategy is better for both entrepreneurs and investors.

You will need second and/or third rounds of financing, and maybe even a very late stage round called a mezzanine. At each of these stages, the existing shareholders and the potential shareholders need to reach agreement about the valuation of the company and that it represents a good opportunity for them both. When new money is put in, if the existing shareholders put in their share of the new money raised, then they maintain their share of the company. If they do not, then their shares are reduced. This is called dilution. Since the second and later rounds are larger with more capital raised, the earlier investors have to find much more money than they put in at first, if they wish to maintain their shares. Since the number of shares owned is related to voting rights, this means that later rounds tend to dilute early investors' shares and votes. As stated by SEC Commissioner:

*Surprising as it may seem, another challenge is how to protect crowdfunding investors when a business actually does well. Angel and venture investors are able to protect their interests through a variety of levers. However, the crowd may be unable, practically speaking, to negotiate for or utilize the same types of levers. As a result, the crowd could see its investments heavily diluted in follow-on offerings.*

*Other Shareholder Incentives.* What else are investors looking for? Other reasons investors might want to buy shares are the following. I am sure you will dangle these incentives in front of your potential investors when they need more than an expected financial return to persuade them.
- Information: .To stay informed of developments in an area.
- Affiliation: To support a cause or company they believe in
- Status: To show how hip they are by being part of the Crowdfunding phenomenon.

It's well-known that some investors in Warren Buffett's Berkshire Hathaway Group pay their $140,000 per share for more than the long-term capital appreciation – they also want to go to the annual shareholder meeting and see the seer himself!

### Building Trust
Clearly you won't get any capital if investors don't think your company is a good deal. For investors to think it's a good deal, they need to believe they will get a decent return, without too much risk, and a better return than they could get elsewhere.

About the time you are ready to go out, there will be a million other small companies trying to do the same thing and inundating potential investors with their prospectuses. How can any investor decide on yours?

The answer is to build trust. Here are several ways to build trust externally for your company:

1. Have trusted people from industry serving on your board. "If Fred is involved, then it must be good." Credibility is all important.

2. Concentrate on high profile investors with a known angle in your field.

3. Get service providers they trust. Good service providers are worried about their reputations and they don't tend to take on work from dodgy clients (not always true) but that is what investors think. Therefore spend some money (real or future money like warrants or promises to use their services) to get some high profile service providers on board. Venture-funded startups in Silicon Valley often attempt to become affiliated with the law firm Wilson Sonsini because of its reputation of being attached to successful companies in the past.

4. Get trustworthy research reports written about your company. What could be better than an independent research house writing a glowing report about you? Cultivate relationships so that they find that writing about you would be interesting to their subscribers.

You can also understand that investors may well be concerned about:

- *Their voting rights*. "Closely-held" companies often have dual classes of stock: those that have voting rights and those with lesser or no voting rights. Common in Europe, but rare in the US until recently companies like Google, Zynga, LinkedIn and Facebook found they could get away with them and employ dual and triple class structures. Being a minority shareholder is not fun for an investor as it is, and having no votes at all can be awful if the shareholder feels the company is not going anywhere. My guess is that, as crowdfunding matures over the next few years, voters will want a "say on pay" (much like today's Dodd Franks Law for public companies). They will also want to weigh in on whether the company can involve itself in ventures they consider far from your original vision. You may find it difficult to raise equity if you don't allow them to have a voice. Until then, they can always sell, of course.

- *Oversubscribing*. Since time immemorial, many promoters have found themselves having offered more shares than are on the register. In other words, some shares have two names on them. Result: investor fraud. Using licensed funding portals or brokers should allay their fears on this front.

## Getting the formal stuff right

It's boring, but it's important to get your ducks in a row, and not take shortcuts. If you are a small business owner already, you will know all this stuff. For those who aren't, here is a quick recap. If you don't get this stuff right, the shareholders (and you) could be sue-able because your failings have allowed outsiders to "pierce the corporate veil," as the expression goes.

- *Company Name*. Choose a name, search for it on the web, check its availability in the trademark website www.uspto.gov, get the domain name, and check on your State's website to make sure no one else has the name. The name should be designed to appeal to investors and customers. It might be best to apply for a trademark at ww.uspto.gov – it would be bad for your credibility if a competitor got it first and you had to sue to get your own name back. (However be aware it can take 6 months to get your trademark approved so don't wait until it is approved.) Realistically, though, something like 73% of all startups change their name in the first year of operation, so there is no need to get too attached to a name. Logo? Sure, why not, but keep it simple!

- *Company structure.* You will need to file for a "C" Corporation. The legalities of the LLC, LLP, and "S" Corporation are not going to be able to handle the needs of so many outside investors. Each of them wants to be protected from legal attack and to have their liability limited to their investment.

- *Legal documents*. Getting the legal paperwork is critical to providing you and your team with protection, while providing investors with what they need. Unfortunately this costs money. In the old days it used to cost $25,000. Nowadays, you can get by with $6,000-8,000. But it is probably more than you thought it would, or should, cost. (I believe there is a need for this to drop and that service providers will emerge to corner this market, see later). There some useful service providers in the "Resources" section.

- *Tax Filings*. The first thing to do is go to www.irs.gov and apply for your EIN (this takes just a few minutes online). Then go to your State Franchise Tax Office and get a State ID (this can take several months but you can start immediately). Pay your application fee (and renew it every year!). When it comes to regular filings, make sure you meet deadlines and pay the fees on-time.

- *Bank Account*. Well, you have to put the money somewhere! You will need your EIN and State tax IDs to open the accounts.

# Summary:
## 2. Setting up a Company Worth Funding

### Getting the Dogs to Eat the Dog Food:
Is this a pain problem or a pleasure solution? Are customers aware of a problem? Do customers accept the product?

### Being Better than the Competition:
Better than existing? Better than substitutes? Is your product defensible?

### Yes, Making Money:
Is customer value greater than costs? Are marketing and overhead costs not overwhelming? Will it recover its startup costs?

### Lifting-Off Quickly:
Can you get rapid customer awareness? Will you achieve rapid customer acceptance? Can you use rapid prototyping? How risky is it? Do you have forgiving margins? Will you overspend before lifting off?

### Building the Team:
Have they worked together before? Does your team have industry-specific knowledge? Is your team adaptable enough to cope with unexpected changes? Do your team members represent all the main core function of a management team?

### Making Your Company Attractive to Investors:
You need to understand how investors think in terms of: survival rates, liquidity, taxes, opportunity costs, expected financial returns, dilution, other shareholder incentives.

### Building Trust:
Have trusted people on the Board. Concentrate on high profile investors. Get service providers investors trust. Get trustworthy research reports written.

### Getting the Formal Stuff Right:
Choose a company name and company structure. Take care of legal documents & tax filings.

# 3.

## Raising the Cash

Raising the cash has several components:
- Choosing Your Funding Portal/Broker
- Valuing the Company
- Setting the Target Funding Threshold
- Marketing to Investors

Let's get started!

**Choosing Your Funding Portal/Broker.** This should be the easy bit! However, you need to make sure you take great care with the regulatory aspects, the information provided to investors, their money and contact details. The JOBS Act requires that you raise money through licensed funding portals or through licensed brokers. There can be much overlap between the two types.

While you could theoretically use an offline broker or portal, and add a web or online presence, it makes sense to use one already on the Internet because of the reduced cost of transactions, the wide availability of information, Regulation Crowdfunding rules (of course), and the ease of taking payments.

The way I see it, you have several options:
- *Existing Crowdfunding Portals*. Your simplest solution is to use existing crowdfunding solutions, like SecondMarket, KickStarter or IndieGoGo. However there is a cost of about 4-9% attached and they may not be regulated or have the full infrastructure at time of writing. Other existing portals are RocketHub and Peerbackers.

- *New Crowdfunding for Startups Portals*. There is room for a series of new portals that focus on Crowdfunding for startups. I expect many to emerge shortly.

- *Home-Made Solution*. An alternative might be to use a ticketing solution like Acteva, or EventBrite; here you set up the classes of shares and any deals you might offer, ask people for their contact details and then collect their credit card details, etc. There may well be regulatory issues, however, if you cannot structure as a funding portal or get regulatory cover through a licensed broker.

- *Existing Public Equity Portal*. In a year or two, the big boys like E*Trade may well be the perfect funding portals. They are regulated, they are on the Internet, they can handle transactions, they list prices, they have a great deal of investor traffic, and they are trusted.

- *Existing Broker-dealers*. Be wary of assuming that investors will be sold on just your marketing materials. The reason we have human salespeople is that they can listen to a customer's desires, respond to objections, and show how their solution solves your needs. This is why stock salespeople still phone you; don't ignore their power. It might well be worth teaming up with an existing stock brokerage; they already have clients and a team to sell your shares.

It is quite possible to use a hybrid of these: maybe with phone salespersons directing traffic to a funding portal. If in doubt, unless you already have a large presence, I suggest going with what is more proven to work. Take care to check the legality of your approach and, if in doubt, avoid the risk of an SEC injunction by going through proven routes.

## Valuing the Company

A famous Harvard Business School Case Study (which you can buy) starts by putting you in the position of a young entrepreneur who is waiting in café for a venture capitalist who he knows will ask him how much of his company he is willing to trade for a million dollars of startup capital. He has a few minutes to figure out how to value his company. You are facing the same issue. How do you solve the problem?

How much to value your company is a tricky issue. If you get it wrong and value it too low, you will work for years and get nothing for your troubles. If you aim too high, you will not receive any money and you will miss an opportunity in the market that your competitors will fill, leaving you nursing your disappointment and regrets. How to judge the right level?

Here's the basic method:
1.  Value the company in 3 years' time
2.  Discount back to get valuation now.

Let's look at these in turn:

### Value the company in 3 years' time

You take your projections for the revenue and profits for where the company will be in three years' time. Then you apply some factors to revenue, profits etc. and come up with a range of figures of the valuation of the company at that time.

So how on Earth to put a figure on the valuation of the company three years hence? Two ways: the first is by considering a company as a machine for producing cash flows; the second is by using comparative multiples. It's important to know about these methods because they can be useful checks on what value you put on the company. The investors of course will be applying the metrics in a similar way!

**a. Cash flow Machine**. Think of a company as a black box. Investment goes in and sometime later investment returns come out. Some boxes are better and faster than others at producing returns. Cash flows are one way of looking at those returns. They are harder to disguise as profit, especially free cash flows (i.e. after depreciation and re-investment in equipment). Of course cash flows will come out into an uncertain future of deep recessions, fierce competition, rising inflation, increasing cost of money, unknown customer demand, optimistic cost ratios and fluctuating investor demand. And the company will not exist forever. This makes it difficult to put a figure on the valuation since half the valuation will be near-blind projection into the future after the third year. It turns out that, while you might feel that a bottom-up valuation like this would be the best, there are so many variables which can vary quite a bit and can be quite esoteric (can you say "weighted average cost of capital" three times in a row?) For that reason and others (not the least of which is familiarity of financiers and their desire for an easy life), most people use comparable multiples, as we will see now.

### b. Comparative multiples.

This technique works by finding a similar or "comparable" company for which you have 2 hard numbers: the valuation and something like revenue (or profit). The latter is known as a "metric". From this you can divide the valuation by the metric to get (in this case) the valuation/revenue figure (="revenue multiple") for that comparable company. This is the famous "comparable multiple." Now all you have to do is look up the same metric (say the revenue) for your company. Multiplying the "revenue multiple" from the other company by the revenue of your company will then give you the valuation of your company. That basic algebra from high school is coming in handy after all!

While a simple concept, it can appear complicated at first so let's consider an analogy. Let's say you want to sell your 2200 sq ft "Craftsman" house with a front garden and 2 car garage; what price should be put on it? The perfect comparable would be a 2200 sq ft "Craftsman" house with a front garden and a 2 car garage around the corner in the same zip code that sold last week, and whose data is public. Assuming you can't find one, however, you have to get as close as you can. Let's say your realtor tells you that the most important factors are floor area and zip code. So you would start to look for houses around 2000-2500 square foot in the same zip code. Most likely you could have to compare your house to:

- A house with 30% more square footage in the same zip code that sold last year
- A house with 10% less square footage in the slightly better zip code next door that sold 2 months ago.
- A house up for sale with the same square footage in a nearby and lesser zip code that may or may not sell for its offering price.

One of the biggest issues is getting a reasonable set of information from the comparable companies. It isn't all public. It is obviously easy enough to project the metric for your company in three years' time (if in doubt, guess.) When it comes to valuing your company, it is going to be a red flag if you show there are 5 exactly comparable companies to yours: they will wonder about your competitive advantage!)

What we confirmed from the house price example is that using comparable multiples is a process of judgment which has two requirements:

- find comparable companies, and
- get metrics on them.

Let's look at the two requirements separately.

*Finding comparable companies.* Ideally you would find a startup that is a perfect clone of yours, for which you have perfect and complete information. The problem comes, when you can't find the metrics you want for companies that are closely comparable, so then you have to find any company vaguely similar to yours that you have some info on!

Typically, you'd take a public company (i.e. it is quoted on a stock exchange and the public can buy its shares.)You can then look up all its metrics, such as price/book value, price/earnings ratio, price earnings growth ratio, price/sales, and then apply those ratios to your company.

Of course being a startup, all you have are projections based on estimates, and you the entrepreneur are optimistic so no one is going to take your figures literally.

Sometimes you are lucky: a private company has just been bought for a certain multiple and the figures are available.

In summary then, here are a few ideas for finding comparables:

- Find a public company in a similar field, preferably a growth company. Then you will have valuation, revenues, profits, everything!
- Look for a private startup you can put a valuation on, and that you have some metrics for. Here are some examples:
  - Just received an investment (received $30m in funding for 30% of the company), so valuing the company.
  - Just been sold (for $35m). Known as an "exit multiple."

- o Just been part of a joint venture with a public company with a share swap.
- o Er, wherever you can find any useful information!

*Choosing suitable metrics.* Clearly what you want are available metrics that investors believe are related to the underlying valuation of their shares. This tends to mean revenues and profits. Here are a few ideas:

- Revenue. Fortunately it is often a source of pride for companies to publish their revenue figures, which means they are often available when nothing else is.
- Profit. Profits are subject to quite varying and opaque policies among comparable companies, and the figures are rarely available for private companies, so revenue forecasts are often easier to use. Of course the purpose of a company is to make a profit, so profit multiples are more persuasive to investors. Sometimes you can talk to people in the industry and get gross margin estimates for similar companies, so you can calculate gross income. Then you can run a spreadsheet to estimate overheads and then get to net income.
- Employees. In the dotcom days, investors used the basic rule of thumb for valuation of $100k for every engineer. The rationale was that it took time to engineer a piece of software and engineers were hard to hire.
- Other esoteric metrics. You can define the debate by inventing your own comparables and coming up with novel rationales for why they make business sense. In the dotcom days they also ratio'd valuations based on number of eyeballs (with the theory being that the more visitors to a website, the more likely they could be converted into paying advertising slots). For software companies with recurring revenue and cross-selling opportunities, the installed base of customers could be relevant. Every industry has its own valuation techniques: retail auto parts retailers often sell at 40% of annual revenues plus inventory, for example. When we sold the company that became E*Trade UK to E*Trade, we used the very metrics they used on themselves in the US!

*Rules of Thumb.* If you are having difficulty finding close comparables, then use general rules of thumb. They are also useful checks on your valuation figures. The following data is from Damadoran Online, a very useful dataset compiled by the NYU Stern Finance Professor.

- *Value/revenue ratios* average 1.7 for all public companies. Often known as Value/Sales Ratios. By industry, they vary between about 0.5 for auto parts, to 0.9 for retail, 3 for software companies, 4 for biotech. Growth companies can have ratios as high as 30, but are typically around 2 or 3.

- *PE Ratios.* (Price/earnings ratio is the price per share divided by the earnings per share, or the value divided by the after tax profits, not that you are likely to be paying tax for a few years). Can be calculated on current, "trailing" (i.e. past), or "forward" (i.e. future earnings), so make sure you compare with the right multiple. In normal conditions, PEs are 8 for mature companies in a recession, rising to about 11 in a boom. Growth companies can rise to 16 to 30 or more. In 2012, coming out of a recession, averages were about 18 on forward earnings. They varied between about 11 for automotive parts to 20 for electronics to about 40 for internet firms.

- *EBITDA Multiples* (Earnings Before Interest and Depreciation and Amortization) and Free Cash Flow (FCF) are also used extensively, as they get closer to the underlying performance of a company without some of the distorting effects of accounting. However you will struggle to get this information for comparable private companies, which means you will be using public company comparables if you want to use EBITDA and FCF. Often referred to as EV/EBITDA multiples, where EV=Enterprise Value which is the value of the equity added to the value of the outstanding debt. Note EBITDA multiples average about 7-8 for public companies, varying between 4 for service companies, 11 for electronics companies, and 22 for e-commerce companies.

*Sample Calculation: Estimate the company value in Year Three*
Here we go. Say your revenue at the end of three years is projected to be $2m. You have managed to find a comparable company that has a revenue multiple of 5 times (i.e. Value/revenue=5.) That means that you could put a value on your company in its third year at $2m x 5=$10m.

In summary, by using comparable multiples and applying them to a similar metric for your company in Year Three, you can estimate the value of your company in Year Three.

### *"Discount back" to value the company now.*
But what does that mean the valuation is now? We need to reduce, or "discount," that value in Year three for risk, time, inflation and opportunity cost over three years, to get the valuation now. In essence, as we will see in a moment, we divide the valuation in three years' time by about 8, equivalent to 100% discount rate every year for three years. Yes, really.

Here's how it works. First of all, consider this analogy. Imagine you had $100 now. Let's say you invested it somewhere and got 100% interest every year for three years, i.e. the money doubles in value every year. (For the financial purists, we will assume it compounds only once a year). This year you have $100. At the end of the year 100% increase takes it to $200. An additional 100% increase over the next year takes it to $400. Now go from year 2 to year 3 and you add an additional 100%, doubling the $400 to $800. In other words, the $100 has become $800. If you went backwards in time then, you would take the expected value in year three of $800 and divide by 8 to get to $100. This is the same, effectively, of discounting the $800 by 100% every year for three years.

So why is this relevant to our trying to discount the valuation in Year three to get it to now, and why did we choose 100% discount rate? Startups are risky, a lot riskier than putting your money into treasuries. What is more, you as an entrepreneur are optimistic and inexperienced and you fudged the figures to give investors what they want. Because of these risks, investors only want to put their money in if there's a chance of high payoff, or a high effective interest rate, otherwise known as the Internal Rate of Return, or IRR, that we have already met. It turns out, that, in general, investors use a rule of thumb of about 100% a year as being what they are willing to go for. That is why we chose 100% (though it also makes the math a lot easier! Which is probably the real reason investors use it, too). (Bygrave's Entrepreneurship book covers this discount rate quite well.)

The valuation of the company today, which we have just calculated by discounting from Year Three, is called the pre-money valuation. As we will cover in more detail in the share price section which follows, this is different from the post-money valuation and it is important that you understand the difference in the next section.

*Sample calculation: Discount back three years to get today's pre-money valuation.* Assume for the moment that investors assume your company to be the usual risky startup for which they would demand an Internal Rate of Return (IRR) of say 100% a year. As we have seen earlier (see financial returns for investors), over a three year period, (when you allow for an annual compounding effect), this means you expect the value of the company to multiply by 8 times. Or, going backwards, they will divide the valuation in year three by 8. (I.e. they would not be willing to assign a figure for today's' valuation higher than $0.25m). Think of it as having $0.25m in a high interest-bearing account earning 100% compound interest for three years, which gets you to $2m.

### Now massage the figures

Since there is quite a range of valuations that can be attached to your company, there is plenty of space to massage the valuation when presenting to investors. Some do this by carefully choice of comparable companies and which metrics to use. Here are some thoughts:

- It is an inexact science. You can produce your spreadsheet, and your potential investors can produce theirs, but the range of values for each assumption is so broad, and the futures so uncertain, that there is realistically no way to put an accurate valuation figure on a startup.

- This simplistic calculation does not allow for the effect of options for the management team, further rounds of capital raised, whether some shares have preferential or priority rights, and any complex securities like convertible debt. Any sophisticated investor will want you to develop a "capitalization table" that projects their dilution and their likely share when you reach the liquidity event.

- One factor that increases comparables is the state of the economy and stock market. If people feel more optimistic, if they allocate money to stocks, if they believe the future is here now, they will bid up valuations, increasing comparable multiples. Obviously, all other things being the same, the time to sell shares is close to a boom, if you can!

- While Crowdfunding for StartUps seems to be mostly American at the moment, you can be sure that other countries will adopt it and extend it if it is successful. Stock markets in different countries often have different values for their multiples, depending on such factors as enthusiasm for stocks, state of development of stock markets etc. This means you will have to look up typical values for multiples in your country.

- Since it is quite difficult to put a figure on a valuation, much depends on circumstantial factors which you as an entrepreneur and booster of your own stock will have to be master of. These include:
    o Whipping up demand for your stock so that demand exceeds supply. That will drive up the valuation.
    o Impressing potential investors with credible figures on the market, and showing how your management team has what it takes to deliver to plan.

### How Much Capital to Raise this Round

There are several parts to figuring out how much cash to raise this round:

- Budgeting your Cash Flows
- Setting the Target Funding Threshold.
- Setting the Share Price

Let's start with what the company needs.

### *Budgeting your Cash Flows*

Obviously the first thing to do is figure how much the company needs to achieve its goals. Therefore you need to budget cash flows, and, in very simplistic terms, that means the three most important things in accounting: incomings, outgoings, and timings.

Keep things simple in the beginning. For every month for the next year or three, project your revenues, add up your expenses, adjust timings, add what cash you started with, and add any cash you can raise. Look at the balance each month. If it is negative it's game over.

Your company might grow so fast that it runs out of working capital. Let's say you are a manufacturer. You will need to buy a full inventory of parts to be ready. You will then need to have an inventory of finished parts, and you will have to wait until you get paid, all of which will suck working capital out of the company. The bigger you become, the bigger the necessary working capital, and it is possible to expense so fast that you outstrip your supply of working capital, which might stop you from getting to the final payment, causing you to run out of cash. Ouch! Therefore timings are important to model. Neil Churchill, Entrepreneurial Finance Professor, calls this the MIFROG calculation: Maximal Internally-Funded Rate of Growth.

Oh, and I should add that you should become an expert at creating scenarios for when things don't go as planned, which they won't! Expect "less revenue, more expenses, and later"! Getting this wrong and being too optimistic is the cause of much heartbreak and wasted effort as financiers take over the company if you run out of cash. Tucker Automobiles in the late 1940s had a revolutionary car but launched before they had spent enough time and money on development and their costs were too close to their revenue to make a decent profit. The EuroTunnel, an ambitious project to cut a railway tunnel under the English Channel succeeded technically, but went bankrupt twice, wiping out all the shareholder equity (including that of the founders).

Now you have an idea of how much money the company will need to make it, and when it needs it. You have some scenarios in case you don't get want you want. The next question is how much to raise for this first round.

**Setting the Target Funding Threshold.**
You obviously don't want to raise too little capital. But you also don't want to raise too much and you definitely don't want to miss reaching your target threshold by aiming too high. The critical question is where to set the threshold. There is a fair amount of judgment involved in setting the threshold. Let's first look at what is normal and then examine arguments for increasing or decreasing the target.

*What is a normal range?*
You probably want to stay within norms to avoid investor problems. Most first rounds from angel investors result in about 30% of the company being owned by them, while investors in some highflying Internet companies end up with only about 8%. In most cases, you should probably aim to offer 15-30% of the present valuation. This is known as the "free float."

*Argument 1: Raise the target*
There are several reasons to go for a higher funding threshold and raise more money.
    a. You are putting in a lot of time and effort and money, so you will want to get your money's worth and raise a good sum.

    b. You have to expect problems and they all take more money to sort out. Customer acceptance may be slower, products may not come out on time, competition may push up the cost of customer acquisition, there may be regulatory holdups, costs will be higher than estimated, and margins may be lower than projected. Having more money means not running out and gives you more time to fix the inevitable problems.

c. Maybe the funding window won't stay open for you. Some will say you can always go back to the trough again, right? Well, maybe...the problem is that investors expect you to reach certain milestones for their first round of returns, and if problems appear and you can't quite make it, they might feel you have lost credibility, or they may already have lost interest.

d. If you do run out of cash, you may find it very time consuming to raise money at a critical juncture. Investors can smell your desperation; they will drive a very hard bargain, if you can even attract their attention at this stage. Running out of money is a cardinal sin for an entrepreneur. One entrepreneur calls it "DROOM: "Don't Run Out Of Money." Undercapitalization is the main form of failure out there.

e. There are two problems with having only a few shares available. The first is that when an investor needs to sell, say because he has to pay property taxes, then he will be so keen to sell that he will accept a lower price than you have been used to. Since the share price is governed by the last price paid, and there is so little traffic in your shares, this can make your share price drop precipitously at exactly the wrong moment. The second reason to go for a higher free float is that if the price is pushed up artificially high because of the reduced supply, then the next round of capital may be a down round. That is, the share price will be lower than before, causing a reduced valuation for existing shareholders, who may therefore resist the second round, limiting your options.

*Argument 2: keep the target lower*
And there are also reasons to go for a lower threshold:

    a. You definitely don't want to miss your target and get no money at all.

    b. You don't want to sell too much equity at too low a price. The earlier stages of a company are riskier. So investors demand a lower price to compensate them. You may feel you know the risks well but investors from the outside don't see things that way, so they will ask for a higher number of shares per dollar to compensate them for their perceived risk. This means you will want to raise the capital in stages so that, as you achieve your goals and get traction in the marketplace, you can sell shares more expensively.

    c. One other advantage of small free floats is that if demand exceeds supply of shares, then the price will rise. This will help raise your profile as having a higher valuation.

Don't forget that you have to take the capital-raising fees from your total raise so you need to allow for that, when setting the target amount of money.

In conclusion, the exercise of setting the target funding threshold is not an easy one, and you should take some experienced advice. Once you have decided how much money to raise in this round, you need to set the share price and issue a certain number of shares. Let's look at that now.

**Setting the Share Price**
There has been a bit of a stigma at having shares priced under $1. In order to keep the share price above $1, we need to:

- Calculate the Post-Money Valuation.
- Issue the Right Number of Shares.
- Calculate a Notional Share Price.
- Calculate How Much you are "Giving Away"

*Calculate the Post-Money Valuation.* A few explanations of the language used here might be useful. Many people get confused

65

when they hear the word "valuation." There are two forms: pre-money and post-money and it is very important to understand the difference between the two. Here, you are projecting your forecasts into the future and you work back to a present valuation of the company. This is the pre-money valuation. Now add the capital infusion and that is the post-money valuation. Why does it matter? The money you raise will entitle your investors to a share of the post-money valuation. If you confuse the two valuation figures, you will be surprised by the shares that investors want.

*Sample Calculation: Calculate the post-money valuation.* Let's say you are looking for $0.1m this round. Ignore any further rounds for the first three years. You remember the pre-money valuation was $0.25m. Then, your post-money valuation would be $0.25+$0.1m=$0.35m.

*Issue the right number of shares*
If the share price is to be above $1, you need to issue a number of shares below the raise. See sample calculation:

*Sample Calculation: Calculate the target share price.* Let's say you issued 80,000 (=$0.08m) shares for this offering. Your target share price will be $0.1m/0.08m shares=$1.25.

*Calculate How Much you are "Giving Away"*
Take the raise and find the percentage of the post money valuation and that is the amount of the company you are trading for the capital infusion.

*Sample Calculation: Calculate the share (of your post-money valuation) your new investors get.* You are raising $0.1m and the post money valuation is $0.35m. So the new investors would be awarded 0.1/0.35=28%.

In summary, you can be sure that your first time around these calculations will not work and you will have to change something and go around again. What is more, just when you think you are ready to go into the world, your potential investors will come back and change the game, see below.

### *Your Investors will Actually Set the Price*

Prices of anything in the marketplace are almost always set by the balance of supply and demand. In other words, everything, including share price, is up for negotiation. If there are several companies like yours out there, or the investors are feeling scared of investing, or do not have very much money to invest right now, or think your company is riskier than you do, then you have to expect a lower price.

What this means is that, using the above calculations, you suggest a share price, then walk out into the marketplace and offer your shares for sale. You then adjust the share price depending on the demand you are finding, in order to raise the money you need for this first round. If you can't get what you need at a price acceptable to you, then you can offer fewer shares for sale; then plan on going back later when you have achieved something to impress the investors.

In traditional offerings, or "private placements," it is the brokers' job to walk around to potential investors in order to gauge demand and prices and start to get commitments from "cornerstone" investors. This is called "building the book." Eventually, usually a short period before the IPO, the share price is set.

### Marketing to Investors

Marketing to investors is one of the hardest parts of the process. With the right offering, you probably could reach investors for very little, but if you have an ambitious goal, are not the first in the field, and don't have a blockbuster, it is going to take time and money. If you expect costs, then you will be more likely to succeed.

I think of 4 major aspects when marketing the deal:
1. The Pitch
2. Pre-Marketing
3. Networking
4. Putting yourself out there

Let's look at each in turn:

### 1.    The Pitch

You need to have something to say, and need to be able to say it persuasively. (Otherwise why bother?)

Whether you deliver your message verbally (the pitch), on paper (the prospectus), or on the web (website), you need to be on message and be able to articulate it in simple terms that grab an investor's interests. There's no point going out into the street and blowing your horn if you don't have a tune people want to hear.

Elevator pitches are a good way to start. As you know, the usual story is that you imagine you step into an elevator with a potential investor. You have five floors to convince him or her to hear more. Three key suggestions are:
- Grab their attention: use a question, say something shocking or surprising.
- Explain the problem and how it is an aspirin used to soothe pain, not a vitamin.
- Illustrate how all the solutions out there are no good, explain how yours is better, and show that people will pay for it.

A prospectus is like a business plan, investment plan and PowerPoint presentation all rolled into one. It is the traditional way to communicate what your company is all about, and you are going to need something like it. Take your elevator pitch and expand that into an executive summary at the beginning. Then structure your prospectus.

The JOBS Act has some limitations about how you can publicize the details of your deal, such as share price, and you might want to keep some details at arm's length from competitors. Clearly, you'll want to have a polished website. You might want to consider an FAQ, and of course don't forget your YouTube video! (Several of the platforms like IndieGoGo offer video upload). Have a simple demo that can be easily accessed.

## 2. Pre-Marketing

Since the time period for raising money can be quite short, you'll want to pre-market your company before you go out formally into the world. This is critical to building marketing momentum.

You may have heard about Casey Hopkins, whose small design company Elevation Lab, used Kickstarter.com to raise money for a new iPhone docking station he had devised. He set out to raise $75,000, reached that target overnight, then doubled his target and went on to raise $1.5m. This made him the first person to break the $1m barrier in a Crowdfunding project. One of the secrets to his success is that he managed to get a ringing endorsement of his product from Wired magazine, which helped persuade some of his more than 3000 customers.

Other pre-marketing ideas include winning endorsements and investments from respected advisers and investors. You'll no doubt have noticed that politicians before an election publish a list of those who support them; you should do the same. You could also write a book (it's easy now and even a 12 page book is useful marketing collateral). And where's your video blog?

When making risky decisions, we first follow people who know, and people we know. For example, when planning a party, it is always a good idea to send your invite out to your closest friends and ask them to RSVP, then send the invite to a larger party list a day later. That way, when the others look at the RSVP list they see lots of names and that persuades them to join. So start now - set up your Facebook page for the company and build up your list of fans; they are your hot hit list.

One of the fastest and most effective ways of getting the ball rolling is through networking, which we will look at now.

## 3. Networking

Just buying ads is going to be expensive and not very effective, so you will have to be smarter – you will have to network to find investors. What is more, you will need to encourage the people you reach to network to others - your first investors will pull in their friends, so encourage them to share your message and sign up.

There are three elements to networking:
- *Affinity Groups*. You need to connect to people who have some connection to you, i.e. with whom you have something in common. Messaging all your 2000 fans on Facebook would be a key strategy. Emailing a group of people you are connected to would be useful: think alumni, hobby groups, meet-up groups, groups of investors.

- *Targeted Individuals.* You need to find ways to reach targeted individuals. Everybody wants a marquee investor or three. They realize that they are popular and are hiding away – they are "dark." To reach them, you can try to go direct or indirectly through connections. Often you have to reach them through referral through intermediaries. (This is another reason why legal advisers like Wilson Sonsini in Silicon Valley are so prized: their connections and willingness to use them benefits all). Is it Kevin Bacon you want? He's only 6 degrees of separation away!

- *Raise your Visibility*. Sometimes you can't direct a message directly at people (you can't find their email address or you have only a push channel between you), so you have to do something that they will find by search engine, something that escapes their filters and slaps them in the face, or something that gets under their radar because it has been recommended by a source they trust. Most important: find the "network spiders." These are the people who know everybody. Once you know them (and impress them) you know everybody.

### 4. Putting yourself out there.
Promotion is one of the hardest parts of the whole capital-raising process, but look at it this way: it used to be even harder when you couldn't tell anyone who wasn't rich about the amazing opportunity your company represents for them!

70

There are perhaps three keys aspects of promotion:
- Marketing Portals,
- PR, and
- Advertising.

In other words, in simplistic terms, this is where you team up with people, do something crazy to get noticed, spend some budget.

a.     *Marketing Portals.* It makes sense to be listed on a site which provides a directory of current Crowdfunding companies looking for funding. The funding portals seem to be prohibited from marketing companies, so they cannot help you with marketing. A marketing portal is one place investors may go to find suitable investments. You will have to provide a listing fee, unless an intermediary uses this as a marketing tool, but almost certainly there will be a "winner-takes-all" effect and one or two players who will emerge as investors can't be bothered to search too many sites on a regular basis, and not many sites will want the liability of doing due diligence on your company, and you will not want to have the hassle of listing on too many sites. The winner will be the first to reach a critical mass through reputation, speed to market, and sheer spending.

b.     *PR.* In essence, "public relations" is all about getting observers to think, write and communicate nice thoughts about your company. These third-party observers are trusted by consumers and investors because you are not buying their words like advertising. They are reporting on what they think their media consumers will benefit from. However, they are also human beings and everyone else is also targeting them. So, unless they have much to choose between you and the next company, they will choose on how they feel about you. So how to stand out as making them feel good? Here are a few ideas:

- Be Helpful. You could provide useful information that people can use. Maybe your website has a collection of useful data. Maybe you commission a survey, or write a white paper. By hard thinking, showing the way things are organized, you can frame the debate in your field, or the way it is looked at. This new way of thinking may well be picked up by industry overseers and give you kudos.

- Be Available. Or, maybe like Hermann Hauser, a prominent entrepreneur, you are always ready to take a call from a reporter and give your opinion from the "grassroots." You can also become known as the person to go to when they need to connect with people in your industry.

- Be newsworthy. Maybe what your company is going to do is conveniently revolutionary in which case you could market your company as being "the first," "the biggest,", or "the most advanced." Or, you could do something more interesting and impactful. You probably don't need to ride a balloon around the world, however! Otherwise expensive parties, colorful lifestyle, unusual clothing, or a catchy name might be enough! Personally, I always ask myself what Steve Jobs, Richard Branson or the Pet Rock guys would do.

c. *Advertising*. The "obvious" answer to getting more awareness is to buy ads on Google Adwords or the like. You will notice, however, that I have deliberately put this promotion technique at the end, to try to persuade you that it is not going to be the most cost-effective route for you and that you should try other avenues first.

Since you will be raising your money through an Internet funding portal of some form, it clearly makes sense to use online promotion. Since there are clear restrictions on direct marketing, most of your non-networked investors are going to find you by searching rather than by you approaching them directly. The purpose of marketing is to provide customers with a product-offering that meets their needs at a reasonable

72

price. Not all investors are the same. Therefore the key is to group, or "segment," these investors and provide them each with a solution that meets their needs. Let's do a thought experiment to segment potential investors. See what you think:

- Equity investors looking for more yield. They are already frequenting the well-known sites, blogs and newsletters for information so you will have to target these publications and media. Then further segment them into those who are considering crowdfunded startups, and those who are not aware of them.

- People in the industry who recognize your company has the solution to a problem they know exists. You can reach them by networking and advertising in the industry and maybe doing a joint venture with an existing company, or vendors in that field.

- Investors who want to experience a crowdfund startup. They are either excited about this new phenomenon in itself or are stimulated by the idea of getting rich quickly like some early Facebook investors.

We in America do like to do our marketing from a stratospheric level: just press the button and the smart bomb advertising hits the target. So convenient. Unfortunately everyone else is thinking the same way, and Google and others are getting very rich while your cost-effectiveness is low and sometimes negative. As in, you are spending more on ads than you are raising in capital. Many businesses have gone bust, planning on spending a decent budget with Adwords, only to find that traffic didn't appear. Be careful about spending your precious pre-investment dollars to raise capital.

Conventional or "offline" promotion also might have its place. Especially among affinity groups which use paper as their communication medium (think alumni magazines), older investors, in person, or where online opportunities are overpriced. I can see students walking around cities with the name of your company temporarily tattooed to their foreheads!

**Summary:**
**3. Raising the Cash**

*Choosing your Funding Portal/Broker:*
Choose between existing crowdfunding portals, new crowdfunding for startups portals, home-made solutions, existing Public Equity Portals, or Existing Stock brokers.

*Valuing the Company:*
Value the company in 3 years time using "cash flow machine" and comparative multiples, discount back to value the company now, then massage the figures.

*Setting the Target Funding Threshold:*
Budget your cash flows, set the Target Funding Threshold, set the share price, but expect that your investors will actually set the share price.

*Marketing to Investors:*
This means: the pitch, pre-marketing, networking, and putting yourself out there.

# 4.

## You have the Cash
## – Now What?

Now that you have a large number in the bank account, I am sure you think that after all that effort raising money, you can relax a bit. Not so! You have four jobs to do:

- keeping your promises
- talking to investors
- managing shareholdings
- raising the next round
- reaching the liquidity event

**Keeping Your Promises**

Now is when you have to spend time building value in the company by meeting all your projections. This is where your ideas of how long things will take, how many customers will buy your service and how quickly, all get tested.

Investors and your family all now expect you to manage the value of the company, and there are several ways of doing this.

*Meeting expectations*. Be massively successful beyond your wildest projections and you won't have any problems. Not so easy, of course. You agreed to tough targets that investors set for your company, and in order to meet them, you are going to have to drive hard and not let up. You must expect to work harder as you fall behind, and keep doing that for years...and keep changing as crises appear. General Patton's famous saying "no plan survives contact with the enemy," shows you need adaptability and willingness to change. "Marines don't plan they improvise."

*Accounting*. Nobody believed your figures before you raised the money, nobody believes them now. And now you are struggling to meet expectations, they know you are going to be putting rosy wrappers round any bad news, or hide it away somewhere. Assuming you are not doing that, it makes sense to spend some money on a reputable auditor since they are seen as holding you more accountable on your figures. We have all seen that auditors can get too close to management and their fees, and their interpretations, but the consequences of not having a credible auditor can be fatal. Look at SinoForest, a Chinese timber group. That analyst group said

76

SinoForest did not in fact control all the assets it said it did. The company virtually went bankrupt as its loans were covenanted on assets and share prices which dropped through the floor. It might not be fun to have that happen to you.

*Managing Rumors.* It would not take much for any mischievous stock investor, or "short," to spread malicious rumors about you. This is a notorious problem for pink sheet companies, especially those that are developing products. They spread rumors that the product is not doing well and the share price drops fast. They make money on put options, or they buy the shares cheap and wait for them to rise.

*Getting to the true underlying performance of a company.* Revenue can be a difficult metric to utilize, especially with a lack of availability of complete documents. Even Enron, a widely revered company with masses of documentation, and Bernie Madoff, with regulators all around him, were able to defraud for many years. But for every bad penny there are good pennies and the key is not to stand too much of a chance of being caught out. There are companies who refused to do business with Madoff because they thought his business model was too good to be true and they were not caught out. You can be one of those too. Here are some things you need to be sensitive of their concerns about:

*Recognizing too much revenue upfront.* If a customer signs a lease on a building and promises to pay every month, how do you account for that? How about a software lease? In the past, companies have tried to recognize all the lifetime revenue in one gulp, right away. But if they have to offer a refund, or the customer walks, then they have over-recognized their revenue. In which case the company can be vastly undervalued, and investors may end up holding worthless paper.

*Never-ending exceptional costs.* "Our profits are a little worse than expected this quarter because of exceptional one-off costs, sorry about that, they will be back to normal shortly" Perhaps. But what if worrying costs are being run through the income statement and these one-off costs are not exceptional or one-offs but regular recurring items. Maybe they indicate tremendous business stress that is destroying the company from within?

Groupon is a recent example of revenue recognition and expense "interpretation." Firstly they chose to remove some hundreds of millions of dollars from their marketing expenses, saying these were customer acquisition costs and were solely necessary to get the business running in its startup phases when lesser marketing efforts would be needed thereafter. (*The Wall Street Journal* called this "financial voodoo.") Secondly they had under-accounted for refund rates, which were much higher than had previously been expected. In both cases, they were forced to restate their earnings, badly diminishing the value of the company.

*Overstating assets*. Some companies claim to own assets they do not, implying a lower capitalization. Perhaps they are owned by associated companies, or by partners. Even if they do hold the assets completely, it is important to make sure the ownership rights are completely transparent and known. Muddy Waters, for example, an investment research house in China, claimed Sinoforest did not actually own all the forest it said it did, and the shares dropped precipitously.

*Personal use of company funds*. Crowdfunding for startups changes many things but this is one line you might not want to cross.

**Talking to Investors**
Theoretically it should be easy to communicate with all those investors. Send them an email message and let them know how nicely their management team is doing in developing kickass projects to wipe out the competition and dominate the world market. Sigh. Unfortunately, it's not going to be like that for several reasons, but there are reasons to be cheerful.

- *You aren't always going to meet expectations.* You know you aren't, the investors know that goals are difficult to achieve, your customers know you may not meet the expectations you've set. Face it. You were selling hard when you raised the money and now things aren't going to plan. You made some promises that can't be kept and you need to say *mea culpa*, things have changed and you have a plan in place to fix the problem and catch up. You could adapt the famous saying of John Maynard Keynes: "When the facts change, I change my mind. What do you do, sir?" You are going need to put a positive spin on it, so you will need a channel to your investors.

- *They want to ask questions*. Sure, you could have someone assigned to communications simply answering emails, but a surprising number will be have to be answered by the top management, and it is going to take a lot of time. Time that could be spent with customers, suppliers and colleagues. You need to find ways to be efficient, yet still accomplish this important task.

- *Your investors will be bitching to each other in public about you*. Yes, they will. And they will expect you to be listening in and commenting. These are always hard situations to deal with because angry people are passionate, not always open, and not always rational. And the fact that they gang up in public to pressure you to get their way makes it difficult for you to present a rosy image to new investors. It is however a result of the open Crowdfunding model which should raise you valuable capital. You have to live with it.

- *You might let them vote!* Your investors might expect that their voice be heard on certain critical decisions. Today, it might even be possible to use an open network like Yahoogroups to run a poll, which you could call a "vote." Either way, you will need to get information to the investors to help them make up their minds and influence them in the way you want.

- *Your competitors are going to be listening in*. Competitors, however, are probably not on the ball, otherwise they would already be doing what you are thinking of doing. Anyway, they will likely wait until you are successful to enter the market because the market may well decide your solution is not going to work.

- *Your shareholders will live far away and never be able to see you and trust you*. How can you gain and maintain trust at a distance? You will have to respond to damaging criticisms. Face it – your company will have some nasty criticism on Facebook, Yelp and Twitter. Ignoring it doesn't seem to work. Corporate platitudes don't seem to work. Low level "sorry, but..." doesn't work. Social media provides an interesting solution to shareholder relations.

- *You will always be marketing to three types of investors*. (Did I mention marketing and selling would be your occupation from this moment on?)

- Existing investors. It's not likely that you will raise all the capital you need the first time, so you will need to get them to invest more in second and third rounds.

- New investors. New investors are important for two reasons: Not all of your existing investors will be able or willing to invest in later rounds, so you will need to add more investors, and later rounds are bigger so you will need more investors to fill the gap.

- Secondary investors. If your investors can't sell their shares then the price will drop and everyone, including you, will be less well-off. This is why car manufacturers allow their dealers to sell used cars: no-one would buy new ones, and people coming in need to be able to trade their old ones.

## Managing Shareholdings

It might make a lot of sense to use a registered transfer agent to manage the company's shareholder book for when investors want to transfer their shares.

## Raising the Next Round

It is very unlikely that you will have raised all you need in the first round, and have become cash positive from customer revenue. That means you will need to do a second round of raising capital.

Any new investor will ask whether the first round investors have invested in the second round. If they haven't, then there is obviously a red flag.

## Reaching the Liquidity Event

Both you and the investors should be keen to make money from the deal. Investors need to reach a place where prices can be reliably put on their shares, and to see a liquidity event to realize returns on their money. There are several ways this can happen:

- *Sale*: Sale is the most common form of shareholder exit. Two typical avenues are these. The company can be sold to another company and the sale proceeds, after debt, are distributed to shareholders. Or, another private equity fund can come in and purchase all the equity.

- *Graymarket*. Pricing of shares can occur by outsiders being able to buy shares from other private investors. Not being public, the company's shares are not listed on an exchange. The best known example of this is SecondMarket.

- *IPO*. Here the company goes public, selling some of its shares in its Initial Public Offering. For a small company, the Over-The-Counter market and the Pink Sheets beckons. The company can also back onto the market using a shell, a company that has either failed but still has its stock market listing, or a company deliberately set up to be the vehicle for a company like yours.

- *Manage the company for dividends*. VCs might call this the "walking dead" but the company still exists and the company equity has value, it just never made it into the stratosphere.

- *Share Buy-Backs*. Use your surplus cash to buy back shares, so increasing the price per share. Effectively handing cash to your investors. Apple is finally doing this after some 30 years in business.

- *Liquidation*. The company sees no reason to continue in business and closes down in an orderly fashion, selling assets and distributing the proceeds to shareholders and debt holders. This could be a precursor to bankruptcy, but could also be because the company was set up to sell one product with a small window of opportunity.

- *Bankruptcy*. The company runs out of cash and declares bankruptcy, in which case all common stockholders stand to lose all their money. The company files to protect its assets while it restructures. If it doesn't emerge, the assets are sold off. And your employees go get jobs working for someone else.

## Summary:
## 4. You have the Cash – Now What?

***Keeping your promises:***
Now you have to: meet expectations, provide accounting, and manage rumors.

***Talking to investors:***
You aren't always going to meet expectations. Investors will want to ask questions, and they will be bitching to each other in public about you. You might let them vote. Your competitors are going to be listening in. Also, your shareholders will live far away and never be able to see you and trust you. Overall, you will be marketing to three types of investors.

***Raising the next round:***
Almost everybody needs more money.

***Reaching the liquidity event through:***
These methods; sale, graymarket, IPO, manage the company for dividends, share buy-backs, liquidation, bankruptcy.

# 5.

## The Future of Crowdfunding for Startups

I believe that Crowdfunding your startup in this new way will become a valid venture capital method, making up 50% or more of all companies funded. But, "making predictions is always difficult," as Yogi Berra said, "especially about the future." So let's take a look at disaster scenarios and then speculate on how it might be. It is all so new that there's probably a bit of each to come!

**It could all go wrong (but we don't think so)**
It seems to be a fact of business life that something good is overexploited to the very fullest extent, beyond all realistic expectations of worthwhile returns. When good results come through, rising prices seem to be self-reinforcing and everybody wants to get involved. Final capitulation of the last surviving doubters leads to a crash. Safeguards are shown to be inadequate, or wrongheaded, or the incentives are so great that people work around them, both legally and illegally. My belief is that Crowdfunding for startups is going to develop and will become a valuable part of the startup funding market.  In the meantime, there are several things that could momentarily halt progress in this direction:

- *Even the usual failure rate.* Inexperienced investors all expect their company to survive and pay back their money. This is just not going to happen.

- *Expecting every company to be out of the ballpark*. Even venture capitalists only have one really good investment out of ten. If you invest in one, you don't have a good likelihood of this one being a big one.

- *Highly publicized scams*. With such mobility and anonymity on the Internet, and euphoria about this new phenomenon, it is inevitable that some investors are going to be taken for a ride.

- *People who can't afford to do so, jump in and lose everything*. Initially it will seem as nobody can fail and people who can't afford to take the hit will put too much into an investment. Even though there are limits to $2000 per person per year for lesser net worth investors, you can be sure that there will always be

86

someone who will hide their investments and really be in for far more. It will either take longer than expected, or it will fail, and they don't have the cash to feed themselves or make their car payments.

- *Diversification doesn't work*. Investors in multiple startups find that sheer diversification in many startups may not deliver acceptable returns, despite apparent "spreading of the risk."

- *Congress could increase the Capital Gains Tax*, thereby reducing returns below what investors find attractive.

- *Massive overregulation in response*.  Faced with an enormous uproar, there will be a call for massive regulation, which will squelch the industry for one or two political cycles.

So, as an entrepreneur, what can you do? Here are a few thoughts:
- Acknowledge these concerns as you talk with shareholders and potential investors. "Yes, I can see that you might be concerned about..." Show how what you are doing is different. "But what we are doing is..." Stand up for Crowdfunding. "And we must all stand up against...."

- Doing a good job in building value and letting shareholders understand that. Get to the liquidity event quickly.

**Speculations on a Bright Future**
So given all that, how might things go in a rosy scenario? Here are some speculations:

- *It will take off when Pension and Insurance Funds enter.* The real action, the thing that will really transform the market is when pension funds are allowed to weigh in and invest. And that will be dependent on the track record of Crowdfunding startups in producing decent risk-weighted returns, whether tax treatment for these investments can be made favorable, and whether the investment mandates imposed on their funds allow them. Regulatory and tax changes are what caused the venture capital industry to explode 40 years ago and would make this market expand enormously.

- *The Venture Capital Boys will muscle in*. I see two developments. The first is that existing venture capital funds may well use crowd funded startups as feeder material for their follow-on investments; the publicity of a successful company will raise their profile tremendously. While there are restrictions on an investment company using crowdfunding to raise money, it might be possible for that company to help its startups raise money through crowdfunding. There is also a restriction on a company raising money to do acquisitions of other companies, unless they are identified beforehand. It's hard to see that someone won't find a way to benefit investors by raising money somehow this way; a sort of CrowdFundVC, perhaps? Investors will find it hard to cope with the deluge of opportunities and will want to outsource the choice and management of those investments. Usually, venture capital funds take several years to raise their capital. Why not crowdfund the capital-raising?

- *Price Discovery by Auction.* It seems reasonable to me that, while we are thinking "crowd," you could combine an eBay/Priceline approach to auctioning off shares to decide their price. The crowd speaks! This will need careful perusal of the Regulation Crowdfunding rules as investors would need to see a price before buying.

- *Differential Share Prices.* Traditionally there have been legal constraints on offering differing share prices to investors. You can't offer a different price for the same thing, but you can offer different prices for different versions of the same thing or if there are concessions. So why not offer a lower price for "bulk purchase:" buy 1000 shares and the price is $0.5/share. Buy 5000 and the price is $0.4/share. You can buy food cheaper by the bulk, why not volume discounts for bigger buyers? Or, the first to subscribe gets a lower price? Make sure you check the current regulations as you may need several classes of shares.

- *Further release of marketing restrictions.* There are some restrictions on how you can market your startup. What if they were opened up? How would that open up the opportunities? Well, to start with it would seem like heaven, but you can be sure that everyone will charge in and it will be even more difficult to differentiate yourself. You must understand that it will cost more money for someone or some service to help you achieve that (hello, Google Adwords!)

- *Non-vanilla securities: Convertibles, derivatives, preference shares.* As people get used to different ways of investing in companies, perhaps we will also have different variants of stocks. Convertible shares are loans or bonds that can be converted to stock, either at the shareholders' wish or the management's decision. They can also be zero coupon, which means the company does not need to use its precious cash to make regular payments (like interest). Preference shares are typically non-voting shares that pay a dividend and have first dibs when there is a liquidation or liquidity event. Derivatives are a hybrid form of security which can allow you to place bets not just on whether the stock goes up or down, or even to safeguard returns if it moves too far from your best guess. Who knows where it might go?

- *Brokers and intermediaries will help startups.* There are so many choices that we become inundated. Investors will need brokers, and startups will need brokers to funnel their shares out to investors.

- *Funding Portals.* The Crowdfunding phenomenon will initially be rather new to people and there is an opportunity for several years for funding portals to match investors and entrepreneurs, by marketing to both. They provide value-added in other ways, such as escrow, investor contact management, shareholding management, and regulatory cover.

- *Measures to encourage longer-term holdings.* It is in your interest to have investors who hang around longer than usual. The JOBS Act makes it harder for investors to sell within the year, but perhaps you could devise something for after that. Maybe offer additional shares (free or reduced price) depending on how long they have held them? This might be possible in the future if you can keep track of who owns what accurately.

- *Escrow services.* The first crowdfunded startups are clearly going to use existing and regulated funding portals. But there may be much scope, given the enormous potential, for doing more of this yourself. In which case you should be able to outsource the money-handling escrow services.

- *Underwriters.* The death of these intermediaries, who provide a guarantee that all the shares will be placed (taking them up themselves if needed to get the issue away) has been predicted for years. But, as Google saw at its IPO, sometimes underwriters may be a necessary evil. With reduced power to dictate high fees, and a lesser burden, reformed underwriters may have a part to play.

- *Hybrid securities.* Knowing the financial services industry, someone is going to come up with a new hybrid security. We tend to think in terms of stocks, bonds and derivatives. I can't help thinking there must be other customized ways of investing. What might they be?

- *Investment Clubs.* The small size of crowdfunded startup deals, and the soon-to-be large number of opportunities, means that investment clubs, existing and totally new, maybe even some specializing in crowdfunded startups, will be big players in this field. They will provide opportunities for entrepreneurs to market their companies, and will provide higher yield investment opportunities for investors while spreading the due diligence costs.

- *Marketing Portals.* Imagine a Yahoo in its early days: a directory of all Crowdfunding deals happening. They can't publish all the details, but they can help potential investors choose. Finders fees might be tricky to set up, but otherwise a subscription model from investors may be a good idea.

**Summary:**
**5. The Future of Crowdfunding for Startups**


***It could all go horribly wrong (but we don't think so):***
Progress may be halted because of: just the usual failure rate of startups, investors expecting the company to fly out of the ballpark,  or highly publicized scams, or people who can't afford to do so jumping in and losing everything, or where diversification doesn't work.  Congress could increase Capital Gains Tax and there could massive overregulation in response.


***Speculations on a bright future:***
It will take off when pension and insurance funds enter, and the venture capital boys will muscle in. What about: price discovery by auction, differential share prices, further release of marketing restrictions, non-vanilla securities, brokers and intermediaries helping startups, funding portals, measures to encourage longer-term holdings, escrow services, hybrid securities, investment clubs,  or marketing portals?

# Useful Resources

### Regulation Crowdfunding final rules

https://www.sec.gov/rules/final/2015/33-9974.pdf This is the easily-readable version, though of 685 pages! All the page references in this book refer to this version. There is also a three-columned version with the same text, which is known as the Federal Register version.

### Books

- *Crowdfunding Bible: How to Raise Money for Any Startup, Video Game or Project;* Steinberg and DeMaria. The big book of all crowdfunding; useful for putting equity funding into perspective.

- *Portable MBA in Entrepreneurship;* Bygrave. Comprehensive and readable book on raising capital from two Babson College professors who have started companies themselves.

- *Guerilla Financing: Alternative Techniques to finance any small business;* Blechman and Levinson. Helpful in putting crowdfunding in perspective and gives advice on how to combine sources of capital.

- *Engineering Your Startup*; Baird. One of the great classic books for entrepreneurs.

- *High Tech Startup*; Nesheim. The other classic book!

- *New Venture Strategies,* Vesper. Good background.

- *New Venture Creation: Entrepreneurship for the 21st Century*; Jeffrey Timmons, Stephen Spinelli. A Harvard Business School Entrepreneurship Professor teams up with a successful entrepreneur.

- *Blue Ocean Strategy*; Kim & Mauborgne. Choosing where you position your startup can mean the difference between swimming in blue water empty of competitors, or in waters that are red with the blood of other players. This book is readable and helpful.

- *Competitive Advantage*; Porter. Understanding what it takes to make money and stay defensible means reading (or, er, maybe skimming) this book.

- *Diffusion of Innovations*; Rogers. Why do some innovations take off quickly, and others take longer? Read this book to find out, and to figure out how to get faster customer acceptance yourself.

- *The Four Steps to Epiphany*; Blank. A hit in Silicon Valley, this book explains that the key is to not ramp up until you have shown by small experiments that customers really want your product.

- *Innovation and Entrepreneurship*; Drucker. The granddaddy of books on innovation. Emphasizes that change is what causes opportunity and lists some ideas to get your juices flowing.

- *Valuation*; Goedhart & Wessel. This is that expensive book by Mckinsey for experts about how to value companies. Surprisingly readable. Probably worth skimming through to understand the terminology and methodology of valuation.

- *The Dark Side of Valuation,* Damadoran. Rather good. Readable, understandable, yet comprehensive.

- *Term Sheets & Valuations: A line-by-line look at the intricacies of terms sheets and valuations*; Wilmerding. Important information you need to understand sophisticated investors if you want them to lead your round of financing. Good explanation of such investor terms such as dilution.

- *Ernst & Young Guide to the IPO Value Journey*; Blowers, Griffith, Milan. Since your company is effectively IPO'ing immediately, this could be a useful primer.

- *Zero to One Million: How to build a company to one million dollars in sales.* Allis. Useful primer for new entrepreneurs.

- *The First Mile: Essentials of Entrepreneurship: What it takes to create successful enterprises*; TIE. An excellent book from TIE, a nonprofit network of entrepreneurs based in Silicon Valley. Highly recommended.

- *The Innovator's Dilemma*; Christensen. The bible for business disruptors.

- *Entrepreneur Journeys*, Mitra. Interviews with entrepreneurs and what really works.

## US Crowdfunding Sites
There are over 500 crowdfunding sites worldwide and I bet a lot of them will be doing crowdfunding for startups shortly!
- Kickstarter; probably the best-known.
- IndieGogo; a popular rival.
- SecondMarket; handled Facebook graymarket pre-IPO
- PeoplesVC.com; an early equity crowdfunding site
- Wefunders
- StartupAddict
- NewJelly.com
- RocketHub
- Peerbackers
- GoFundMe
- FundaGeek
- Start.ac

## Foreign CrowdFunding sites
- FundedByMe.se (Sweden)
- CrowdCube.co.uk (UK)
- Pozible (Austria)
- CrowdAboutNow (Netherlands)

## Valuation and Investing sites
- Investorpedia.com; good information about investing
- BizBuySell.com; a source of comparable multiples
- BVResources.com; business valuation information
- Damadoran Online; datasets on multiples

**Legal Documents**
- RegDResources.com; a good starting-point for legal documents
- LegalZoom.com

**Research into the CrowdFunding phenomenon**
- Crowdsourcing.org; a good source of up-to-date info on the various segments of the crowdfunding and crowdsourcing field.

**Blogs**
- DailyCrowdSource.com
- ValleyWag; a view into Silicon Valley
- TechCrunch
- Mashable; especially good articles on crowdfunding
- VentureBeat
- 47Hats
- Boing Boing

**Magazines**
- Entrepreneur; always a good place to go to keep up-to-date
- Fast Company

**Associations**
- National Crowdfunding Association (US)
- International Crowdfunding Association
- European CrowdFunding Association
- European CrowdFunding Network
- American Association of Individual Investors
- SCORE

# Index

# Other Books by Rupert M. Hart

"Recession Storming: Thriving in Downturns through Superior Marketing, Pricing and Product Strategies," 2008, 2011. Originally "Competitive Opportunity: How to Achieve Successful Business Performance in Hard Times", Kogan Page,1992

"Effective Networking for Professional Success", 1995.

Technology Venture Capital Directory, 1999.

"Guide To the Stimulus: The Definitive Desk Reference to the American Recovery & Reinvestment Act," 2009.

"Recession 101: Understanding the Business Environment in Recession and Recovery," 2009.

"Cutting Costs Effectively in Recession & Recovery," 2009.

"Maximizing Revenue and Margin from your Existing Customers in Recession and Recovery," 2009.

"Resisting Pricing Pressure in Recession and Recovery", 2009.

"Advancing with New Product-Offerings in Recession and Recovery", 2009.

"Winning New Customers in Recession and Recovery," 2009.

"Making Acquisitions in Recession & Recovery," 2009.